HOW TO SEE IN THE SPIRIT REALM, EVERY DAY

- It is your birthright

By

R.K. Ali Bocus

HOW TO SEE IN THE SPIRIT REALM, EVERY DAY – It is your birthright

ISBN: 9798871794876

Copyright © 2023 R.K. Ali Bocus

All rights reserved. No part of this book may be reproduced, stored in a retrieval system, or transmitted by any means, electronic, mechanical, photocopying, recording, or otherwise, without written permission from the author.

Unless otherwise indicated, all Scripture quotations are taken from the King James Version of the Bible, The Message Bible Translation and The Amplified Bible Translation Version, Classic.

Dedication

This book is wholly dedicated to the Lord Jesus Christ whom I have been serving since Childhood. I have written this book in obedience to Him, for all believers in Christ to be drawn into a closer relationship with Him, and experience what actually belongs to them as residents of the Kingdom of God.

We are living in crucial times, and it is absolutely necessary for all believers to be able to see, hear and discern very clearly and accurately what is taking place in the spirit realm.

Special Thanks

I also give special thanks to my wife for her continuous, loving support and encouragement which has helped me to complete the writing of books, and to do the will of God.

Table Of Contents

Chapter 1	Be Pure in heart	19
Chapter 2	Transforming of your Soul	41
Chapter 3	Develop a Love-Relationship with the Lord Jesus Christ	59
Chapter 4	Be Still – Practice being still	74
Chapter 5	Instant and Complete Obedience	80
Chapter 6	Love not the World	89
Chapter 7	Live a sinless life	101
Chapter 8	Fasting & Prayer	119
Chapter 9	Sanctify yourself	155
Chapter 10	Speaking in Tongues	173
Chapter 11	Walking in the Spirit	183

Chapter 12	Seeking the Lord	233
Chapter 13	How do I know if I am hearing from God or not?	239
Chapter 14	Pray these Prayers	241

HOW TO SEE IN THE SPIRIT REALM, EVERY DAY - It is your Birthright

My friend, do you ever wish you could see in the spirit realm like others have?

Do you desire to see angels, heaven, The Lord Jesus Christ, and have other meaningful, spiritual encounters?

Do you know you can?

Do you know it is your birthright as a born again believer in Christ to have these experiences and more?

When God made man He made man to have fellowship and face-to-face communion with Him, every day, but as you know, that communion was broken when Adam and Eve sinned.

However, do you know that His purpose for making man has not changed because Adam and Eve fell into sin in the Garden of Eden?

It is still the same.

He still wants to have that kind of one-on-one fellowship with you, as He did with Adam and Eve in the Garden of Eden.

This is why He has made provisions (through the death and resurrection of Jesus Christ) for us to have that kind of fellowship with Him restored.

The main purpose of this book is not just to get you to pursue seeing in the spirit realm, but to foster in you a deep desire and hunger to know the Lord Jesus more and more, then, as a result of your close fellowship with Him, He would allow you to see in the spirit realm....He would activate your spiritual senses, as a by-product of knowing Him.

As you read this book, I pray that the Holy Spirit would stir up such a yearning in you to know the Lord Jesus Christ more and more, to draw closer to Him, and to experience what it means to be one with Him. And once you make these intentions your life's purpose and pursuit, then, seeing in the spirit realm becomes natural and automatic. You will not even need to pray for it, it would become a natural benefit in your quest to know Him.

Now even though this book does reveal thirteen (13) patterns and procedures which myself and certain believers had implemented and seen in the spirit realm, please focus on developing an intimate relationship with the Lord Jesus Christ, first.

My spiritual senses were activated because I pursued Him, first.

My friend, God wants you to see in the spirit realm more than you want to see in the spirit realm.

However, seeing in the spirit realm is not entirely up to God, without us having some form of input to cause these dimensions to open up to us. We cannot relegate these experiences completely to God; and say 'it is up to God'.

"If God wants me to see in the spirit realm, He will just allow me to see. I don't have to do or cannot do anything which would open up that realm to me."

That is not true.

You do have an active role to play in your spiritual senses being activated for you to see in the spirit realm.

And although God can and has sovereignly allowed certain believers to see in the realm of the spirit without any seemingly active input from those individuals, that is not the norm for every believer.

While God can open up the spirit realm to you sovereignly without any effort on your part, He does not. Although it is His will for you to see in the spirit.

This right to see in the spirit is conditional like so many other promises of God in His Word.

If you meet these conditions, and stay clear of all hindrances blocking your spiritual sight, you will see in the spirit realm with ease, every day.

This is how He made you to function.

He made you with the ability to function in both the physical and spiritual worlds at the same time.

You already have the resources, design and ability to see, hear and function in the spirit realm resident in you, just like a bird already have the ability and physical make-up to fly inbuilt in them.

God already made you to operate in both the natural and spiritual realms simultaneously. You don't have to struggle to function this way.

Most people don't operate on these levels because they have allowed their mind, will and emotions (their soul) to get in the way.

But God has specifically made you with a spirit, soul and body for that reason – To operate in and interact with both realms at the same time.

This is why He gave you a spirit, it is for the purpose of seeing, communicating, and operating in the spirit realm while on earth.

This is why He gave you a soul and body. It is for the purpose of seeing, communicating and functioning in the physical world He created.

And finally, this is why He gave you a spirit, soul and body; it is for the purpose of seeing, communicating and living in both the spirit realm and the physical realm at the same time, every moment of every day.

So it should be natural for us to see in the spirit realm all the time. This is what He wants us to be able to do. This is how He made us to live. He made us with the ability and capacity to live like this. This should be our natural habitat - Not something to fear, but to embrace.

He has made available to us a gift to a world of limitless possibilities, spiritual encounters and heavenly experiences.

What we need to do is learn how to function in our highest potential in these both realms: Physical and Spiritual realms.

(A realm is a community or territory over which a sovereign rules)

Both the physical and spiritual realms are places where Almighty God rules. These are the realms in which He made you to freely, easily, consciously and naturally interact.

Many times we have experienced moments, been to places, witness events transpired, met people, etc., which we strongly felt we have experienced, met or witnessed before, but just can't remember the details of it.

We have termed those experiences, **déjà vu**. But really, these experiences happen to us more often than we can recall.

Believe it or not, every day we do operate in these realms in a limited way, but He wants us to supersede and excel in the realms He has equipped us to fulfill our roles and destiny in.

My friend, you don't have to wait until you die before you can see in the spirit realm, or before you can see the Lord Jesus Christ, or visit heaven, or see the angels of God.

Why do I say this?

Because once you are born again, you are translated out of the kingdom of darkness into the kingdom of His dear Son, immediately.

How can you be part of this kingdom and not see this kingdom?

The Lord Jesus Christ, Himself, said if you were born again you would see the kingdom of God.

Jesus answered and said unto him (Nicodemus), Verily, verily, I say unto thee, Except a man be born again, he cannot **see the kingdom of God.** John 3:3

The bible also states that we are ambassadors of the kingdom of God.

2 Corinthians 5:20 King James Version
Now then we are **ambassadors** for Christ, as though God did beseech you by us: we pray you in Christ's stead, be ye reconciled to God.

How can we be an ambassador of the kingdom of God and not have access to visit or see it, until we die?

The bible also states that we can come boldly to the throne of God and find grace to help in the time of need.

Hebrews 4:16   King James Version

Let us **therefore come boldly** unto **the throne** of grace, that we may obtain mercy, and find grace **to** help in time of need.

How can we come boldly to the throne of God and not see in the spirit realm, not see Him, angels or the saints of God there?

The Word of God states that as many as received Him to them gave He power to become the sons of God, even to them who believe on His name.

John 1:12

But as many as received him, **to** them **gave He power to become** the sons of God, even **to** them that believe on his name:

How can we be sons and daughters of God and not be able to see our Heavenly Father or the Lord Jesus Christ, Himself?

The bible states that we are citizens of heaven, residents of the kingdom of God.

Ephesians 2: 18, 19 King James Bible

[18] For through him we both have access by one Spirit unto the Father.

[19] Now therefore ye are no more strangers and foreigners, but fellowcitizens with the saints, and of the household of God;

How can we be citizens of heaven and not visit or see heaven, the angels, the King of Heaven and the Heavenly Father?

Amplified Bible Classic Version

Ephesians 2: 18, 19

[18] For it is through Him that we both [whether far off or near] now have an introduction (access) by one [Holy] Spirit to the Father [so that we are able to approach Him].

[19] Therefore you are no longer outsiders (exiles, migrants, and aliens, excluded from the rights of citizens), **but you now share citizenship with the saints (God's own people, consecrated and set**

apart for Himself); and you belong to God's [own] household.

My friends, seeing in the spirit realm is your birthright, don't settle for less than what He has provided for you.

Don't settle for anything less.

There are reasons why you are not seeing in the spirit realm as clearly as you are seeing the natural realm.

This book deals with those hindrances head-on.

Read it with your heart involved, and genuinely put into practice its teachings, and you will discover that the unseen realm will open up to you.

Chapter 1

Be Pure in heart
– the pure in heart shall see God

Blessed are **the pure in heart for they shall see God**. Matthew 5:8   KJV

[3] Who shall ascend into the hill of the LORD? Or who shall stand in his holy place?

[4] **He that hath** clean hands, and **a pure heart**; who hath not lifted up his soul unto vanity, nor sworn deceitfully.

Psalms 24: 3, 4   KJV

The pure in heart shall see God, the Word of God promises. This is not a promise for the hereafter, but for now.

We have mistakenly postponed this promise for when we die and go to heaven, but Jesus meant the pure in heart will see God, here and now, while they are alive on earth. Because we have been taught wrong about this verse we have not experienced its promise.

Of course, this is a conditional promise reserved for the pure in heart – They shall see God

What does it mean to be pure in heart?

What does the word 'Pure' mean?

When you hear the word 'Pure' what comes to your mind?

For instance, if you go to the grocery and pick up a bottle of water which states on the bottle that this is 'Pure' water.

What does that mean to you?

What is the opposite of 'Pure'?

Stay with me here, I am lingering on this because I want you to get a clear picture and understanding of what the Lord means when He says 'the pure in heart shall see God'.

The opposite of 'Pure' is impure. It is something which is contaminated with harmful chemicals or products.

This is the meaning of the word 'Pure' according to the Merriam-Webster Dictionary

(1) unmixed with any other matter

(2) free from dust, dirt, or taint

(3) SPOTLESS, STAINLESS

This is what the Lord Jesus Christ wants for His Church, His Bride. This is what the Lord Jesus Christ wants:

- Spotless believers

    Who are free from dust, dirt or taint,

- And who are unmixed with any other thing which is not a part of His character.

'Pure in heart' means to be clean and holy in all your words, thoughts and deeds every day. It means being purer than a one-day old baby.

This is one reason why children tend to see in the spirit realm easier than adults. It is because they are innocent and has a measure of purity in their heart.

1 John 3:2-4   King James Version

² Beloved, now are we the sons of God, and it doth not yet appear what we shall be: but we know that, when he shall appear, we shall be like him; for we shall see him as he is.

³ And every man that hath this hope in him purifieth himself, even as he is pure.

It says, 'every man….purifies himself, even as He is pure'.

The Word of God is saying that you have a responsibility to 'Purify Yourself' even as He is Pure.

What does that mean?

How can you purify yourself?

By removing or getting rid of everything that is impure. By getting rid of everything that contaminates. By removing everything within you that is not of God – that you will not find in heaven.

For instance, is there lying, cheating, cursing, hating, slandering, gossiping, smoking, gambling, violence, fornication, adultery, etc. in heaven?

No, none of these things are?

Therefore, if it is not in heaven, then to be pure means to remove these things and any other thing which would not be found in heaven from your life.

How does someone become pure in heart?

What does it take for someone to become pure in heart?

What does someone have to do to become pure in heart?

Purity of heart has to do with your words, thoughts, intentions or motives, and deeds

To become pure in heart you would have to get rid of each of the following characteristics.

You would have to walk, live and be free from each of the following sins and only demonstrate the fruit of the Holy Spirit.

Sad to say, there are believers in the Lord Jesus Christ who practice the following works of the flesh.

To see clearly in the spirit realm, particularly the heavenly spirit realm, you would have to be free from:

- ✓ **Unforgiving and hateful thoughts in your heart towards others.**

The Holy Bible states if you hate someone in your heart you are a murderer.

[15] Whosoever hateth his brother is a murderer: and ye know that no murderer hath eternal life abiding in him.

1 John 3:15 King James Version

Now please note, that forgiving someone does not mean that you would have to become buddy-buddy with them. Particularly, if they were an abusive person.

What do I mean by this?

There are some people who are not good company to keep (although you forgave them for whatever wrongs they had done to you) because of the things they practice, and their overall conduct or character.

- ✓ **Adulteries**

You may think, I have not committed adultery, but have you ever looked upon a man or woman who is not your wife or husband and secretly lusted for them in your heart? Or, have you ever wondered and imagined what it would be like to be married to someone who is not your husband or wife?

Believe it or not that is called adultery in God's eyes.

One usher from a local assembly confessed to a fellow-believer who left her husband to be with him that had been looking at her for a long time, secretly wishing, longing and lusting after her – silently wishing in his heart that he could be with her.

In Matthew 5: 27, 28 King James Version Jesus said:

> ²⁷ Ye have heard that it was said by them of old time, Thou shalt not commit adultery:
>
> ²⁸ But I say unto you, That whosoever looketh on a woman to lust after her hath committed adultery with her already in his heart.

There are two (2) kinds of adultery existing in the world today: External and Internal Adultery.

External adultery is actually committing the physical, sexual act with someone who is not your wife or husband, even if no penetration took place – even if it was just oral sex. It is still adultery if it was with someone who is not your wife or husband.

Internal adultery is desiring, imagining or longing to

be with someone on the inside of you, in your heart and your soul, who is not your husband or wife.   .

- ✓ **Fornication** – Being single and having sex outside of marriage is called fornication. Please note, as a single person, you can also have fornication with someone in your thoughts using your imaginations or by watching pornography. This is also fornication..

- ✓ **Stealing**

- ✓ **Sexual immorality –** pedophilia, bestiality, homosexuality, lesbianism, bi-sexual lifestyle, adultery and fornication, masturbation, watching pornography, sexually fantasizing about someone who is not your husband or wife…

- ✓ **Lying**

- ✓ **Deceit**

- ✓ **Cursing** – I am particularly talking about wishing others harm, loss, wrong, or bad things; calling others names that are word curses. E.g. Names like fool, stupid, loser, good-for-nothing…

- ✓ **Thinking wrong, unloving and evil thoughts of others**
- ✓ **Speaking unloving words of others inwardly and outwardly.**

Slander – this is speaking false words of a person to others with the intention of smearing or destroying their reputation; or making them appear bad or terrible in the eyes of others.

According to the dictionary, slander means the action or crime of making a false spoken statement which is damaging to a person's reputation.

It is Malicious gossiping of someone.

It is telling lies about someone with others.

It is backbiting - The word backbiting comes from the Middle English word **backbite**, meaning to speak unfavourably or slanderously of a person who is not present ~ www.dictionary.com

Slander is false accusation.

It is bad mouthing.

It is giving a false report of another.

It is speaking evil of and insulting another, and giving them a bad name.

✓ Pride

Proverbs 16: 18   KJV states that:

Pride goeth before destruction and a haughty spirit before a fall.

And in the book of James 4:6, it says

…Wherefore he saith God resisteth the proud, but giveth grace unto **the** humble.

✓ Foolishness

Proverbs 24:9 says that the thought of foolishness is sin: and the scorner is an abomination to men.

What is foolishness?

What are biblical examples of foolishness?

When Job's wife told him to curse God and die, after he lost everything and was scraping the itching sores on his body with pieces of broken pottery to find relief, he replied to her "You speak like one of the foolish women.

Job 2: 8 – 10

Another example of foolishness is found in the book of psalms where it is written; the fool had said in his heart there is no God,

The fool hath said in his heart, **there** is no God.

Psalm 14: 1   KJV

- ✓ **Abusiveness**

- ✓ **Uncaring Attitudes –**

Luke 11:46   KJV

And he said, Woe unto you also, ye lawyers! for ye lade men with burdens grievous to be borne, and ye yourselves touch not the burdens with one of your fingers.

- ✓ **Coveting & Envying** – strongly desiring what belongs to someone else.

Matthew 12: 13 - 15

¹³ And one of the company said unto him, Master, speak to my brother, that he divide the inheritance with me.

¹⁴ And he said unto him, Man, who made me a judge or a divider over you?

¹⁵ And he said unto them, Take heed, and beware of covetousness: for a man's life consisteth not in the abundance of the things which he possesseth.

- ✓ **Sarcasm** – what is sarcasm?

What is an example of sarcasm?

Have a friend or relative whom you haven't seen for some time ever said this to you when they did see you?

"Stranger!"

"I say you migrated and went to the U.S. to live."

Sarcasm is not of God. If you are a sarcastic person you are not being witty with your words, you are being ungodly.

Let me ask you a question.

"When someone is being sarcastic to you, personally, do you like it?"

Do you feel encouraged or uplifted by it?

Well, what you don't like for yourself, don't do to others.

✓ **Verbal manipulation**

Here is an example of verbal manipulation:

"When are you coming to visit me? When ah dead?"

When someone says this, they don't realize that they are trying to verbally manipulate you, and verbally force you to visit them.

Do you know that all forms of verbal manipulations are wrong?

Here is another example:

"After all the things I did for you, you cannot do this one thing for me?"

To be pure in heart means not thinking wrong thoughts or internally saying wrong words about others; and not doing things for others with wrong and selfish motives.

Matthew 7: 20 – 22   Amplified Version, Classic

[20] And He said, What comes out of a man is what makes a man unclean and renders [him] unhallowed.

[21] For from within, [that is] out of the hearts of men, come base and wicked thoughts, sexual immorality, stealing, murder, adultery,

[22] Coveting (a greedy desire to have more wealth), dangerous and destructive wickedness, deceit; unrestrained (indecent) conduct; an evil eye (envy), slander (evil speaking, malicious misrepresentation, abusiveness), pride (the sin of

an uplifted heart against God and man), foolishness (folly, lack of sense, recklessness, thoughtlessness).

²³ All these evil [purposes and desires] come from within, and they make the man unclean *and* render him unhallowed.

How do I become pure in heart?

Do the opposite of what is outlined above and you will become pure in heart.

Here is how you do this:

- Think loving thoughts of the Lord Jesus Christ all the time.

- Think only loving thoughts of others all the time.

- Use your inner and outer words to bless others. Always bless others with your words inwardly and outwardly.

Example: If someone who had done you wrong and offended you, comes to your mind, say, outwardly with your mouth and inwardly in your thoughts, "Lord, I bless (call their name here) in the name of the Lord Jesus Christ."

- Think highly of others.//
- Only keep a Godlike-view of others.
- Do not think prideful thoughts, better-than-others thoughts, or thoughts which look down on others.

Question:

Wouldn't people take advantage of you if you are pure in heart?

Answer:

The Lord Jesus said in Mark 9:42   KJV

And whosoever shall offend one of these little ones that believe in me, it is better for him that a millstone were hanged about his neck, and he were cast into the sea.

In summation:

How do you become pure in heart?

You become pure in heart by ensuring you are guileless, and clean, in:

- ✓ What you think
- ✓ What you read
- ✓ What and Who you listen to
- ✓ What you watch
- ✓ What you say
- ✓ What you do

Purity of heart is also dependent on who you associate yourself with.

Purity of heart is the state of being restored to what Adam and Eve were like before they sinned.

This state I am speaking of is even purer than that of a new born baby which do not know right from wrong.

Why do I say so?

Because, even though a new born baby has no

knowledge of or experience with sin, they were still born with a sinful nature because of Adam's sin. Since the Word of God states we were all born in sin and shaped in iniquity, and in need of a Saviour and salvation.

Because Adam & Eve were pure in heart, God was able to come down in the cool of the day and have personal fellowship with them…to talk to them face-to-face, like He did with Moses in the wilderness. It's because they were pure in heart – sinless. They were so pure that they did not even know they were naked.

They did not know anything about hate, backbiting, fear, lust, pride, envy, malice, unforgiveness, deceit, bitterness, thinking wrong thoughts about others, drunkenness, racism, adultery, fornication, stealing, murder, crime, etc.

"Can I become pure in heart like Adam and Eve were before they sinned?"

Yes, you can.

The Lord Jesus Christ already paid the price for you to be able to have access to the Heavenly Father, and He also gave you His Holy Spirit to help transform you (as a born again believer) into the image of Christ – Pure and Sinless.

Please note though, this is a process and it does not happen overnight. But you must constantly desire to be pure in heart, daily ask Him to make you pure in heart, and do the things which He has instructed you to do in His Word which will make you pure in heart.

Here is a question you need to ask yourself to determine if you are pure in heart?

"How does someone who is pure in heart see or think of others?"

They see them as having no guile in them.

Isn't that true of a baby?

Does a baby have any ill-thoughts or feelings toward anyone, saved or unsaved, good or bad?

Do you understand now why Jesus said the "Pure in heart shall see God?"

Exercise:

I want to you to identify someone who had done you wrong, someone who had offended you in one way or another.

Have you done that?

Can you see that person in your mind now?

Okay, what I want you to do is to sincerely pray the prayer below for them.

"Heavenly Father, I ask you to bless (call their name here) in their going in and their going out. I ask you to bless their food basket. I ask you Heavenly Father that you would do them good. I ask that you would bless them with the blessing of the Lord which makes rich and adds no sorrow with it, in the name of the Lord Jesus Christ I pray. Amen."

Have you completed your exercise?

Good.

Now I want you to identify another person who had done you wrong and offended you; and I want you to repeat the exercise, praying the same prayer for them.

Practice this exercise daily for 35 days straight. Praying for the same individuals you have identified as persons who had done you wrong or offended you in one way or another, until you only think good things about them…until the thought of them only brings good feelings in your heart towards them.

Happy exercising!

Chapter 2

Transforming of your soul
– your soul needs to be transformed

The soul, which is the mind, will and emotions of a person, needs to be totally transformed to see completely, clearly, accurately, consistently and continuously into the realm of the spirit.

Please read the previous sentence over and over until you get a revelation of its meaning.

When you receive the Lord Jesus Christ as your Saviour:

- Your spirit is saved,
- Your spirit is cleansed from all sin, and the power and control of sin,
- Your spirit is reconnected with the Heavenly Father.
- Your spirit is translated from the kingdom of darkness into the kingdom of God.

What does not happen when you receive Christ as your Saviour is your soul is not transformed and your body is not redeemed.

Salvation is tri-fold in nature - 1 Thessalonians 5: 23

It consists of:

1. **Saving of your spirit.** Acts 16:30, 31; Romans 10:9, 13; Ephesians 2: 8,9; Acts 2: 21; Acts 4: 12; Acts 15:11; 1 Corinthians 5:5

2. **Transformation of your soul** – your mind, will and emotions. Romans 12:2; 2 Corinthians 10: 4 to 6

3. **Redemption of your body.** Romans 8:23; 1 Corinthians 15: 47 to 58; 1 Thessalonians 4: 13 to 18

We have an active role to play in the second part of Salvation, which is, the Transformation of our soul.

- ✓ Your soul consist of Your Mind – which generates and harbours your thoughts and imaginations.

- ✓ Your soul consist of Your Will, which contains Your Power to Choose – Your Power of Choice.

- ✓ Your soul consist of Your Emotions - Your feelings.

When you were born again only your spirit was saved. Your soul which consists of your mind, will and emotions are not automatically transformed. They still need to be transformed.

How is the soul transformed?

The answer to that question is found in:

2 Corinthians 10:4 to 6 and Romans 12: 1, 2

2 Corinthians 10:4 to 6 King James Version

[4] For the weapons of our warfare are not carnal, but mighty through God to the pulling down of strongholds;

[5] **Casting down imaginations**, and every high thing

that exalteth itself against the knowledge of God, **and bringing into captivity every thought to the obedience of Christ**;

⁶ And having in a readiness to revenge all disobedience, when your obedience is fulfilled.

Romans 12: 1, 2 King James Version

12 I beseech you therefore, brethren, by the mercies of God, that ye present your bodies a living sacrifice, holy, acceptable unto God, which is your reasonable service.

² And be not conformed to this world: but **be ye transformed by the renewing of your mind,** that ye may prove what is that good, and acceptable, and perfect, will of God.

How is your soul transformed?

– Your soul is transformed by bringing every thought and imagination which comes to your mind, every moment of every day, into obedience to Christ. By focusing all your thoughts and imaginations which comes to your mind on the Lord Jesus Christ and the Word of God every moment, every second, every minute, every hour of every day, week, month and year.

- Your soul is transformed by having your mind renewed.

How is your mind renewed?

You renew your mind by filling it with the Word of God; and having the Word of God govern your way of thinking, your emotions and your Power of Choice.

What does this mean in plain English?

It is said that the average person thinks approximately 70,000 thoughts a day. Transforming our soul literally means causing those 70,000 thoughts to be only thoughts that are pleasing to God, every moment of everyday – 24 hours a day, every day, 7 days a week, every week, 30 days a month, every month, and 365 days a year, every year.

This is how the soul is transformed.

I know that may appear to be a very tall task to accomplish, but it is possible to accomplish that. Believe it or not.

You are not under the control of your thoughts, but your thoughts are under the control of you.

You are not a helpless victim, or a passive bystander to the thoughts which come to your mind.

God has given you the Power of Choice. He has equipped everyone with that Power, which means you can actually use that Power, the Power of the will to choose what you want to think every moment of every day.

You can start this process by practicing for thirty (30) minutes or more a day, where you focus all your thoughts (let it be love thoughts) on the Lord Jesus Christ alone.

Don't think about anything else during this time.

It will require consistent practice to fully achieve this, though.

When your spirit is saved and your soul (your thoughts, imaginations, will and emotions) is transformed, and your body is fully yielded to God – seeing in the Spirit becomes effortless and automatic.

What is the purpose of your soul?

God has designed your soul to be the bridge between your body and spirit. It is the medium through which the Holy Spirit can find expression and legal right to function in this world. And it is the door through which your body can connect with the Spirit of God and the spirit realm.

Your soul allows this 2-way traffic between the Holy Spirit and the body. It facilitates the body connecting with the Holy Spirit; and the Holy Spirit finding expression in the physical realm through the body.

This is also why demonic spirits seek to influence and take control of your soul. It is because they know if they can take control of your soul through their influences (through the influences of their words, pictures and doctrines) they would be able to 'legally' carry out their evil intentions and plans for the earth and mankind.

YOUR SOUL IS THE BRIDGE TO YOUR BODY & SPIRIT

BODY | YOUR SOUL IS THE BRIDGE TO YOUR BODY AND SPIRIT / SOUL | SPIRIT

❖ He has made the soul to connect the spirit of a person to the natural, physical realm;

❖ And He has made the soul to be able to connect the physical body to the spirit realm.

With your soul you could know, understand, contact,

explore and interact with both the physical world and the spiritual realm at the same time.

However, because the spirit realm is limitless in its dimensions, and the physical realm is also massive, (this includes the universes, and the seen and unseen physical realms), it would take you more than a lifetime to know, understand and explore them all.

Actually, it would take you eternity to fully discover and traverse these worlds.

You need your soul to be able to connect with both of these huge worlds: the spiritual world and the physical world.

Why am I sharing this with you?

I am sharing these facts and truths with you because believers in Christ have been living way below what He has already provided for us.

Not only are the physical realm and the spiritual realm (the heavenly spiritual realm) enormous, but do know that even your spirit, which is in you is huge?

How do I know that?

Because if a spirit called legion, which consisted of about 2,000 – 6,000 devils (a legion in the times of the Roman Empire when Jesus walked the earth comprised about 2,000 – 6,000 soldiers), could have comfortably lived in one man, a man from the country of the Gadarenes, then the human spirit is very large to contain this amount of evil spirits.

On the good side, the human spirit had to be very vast to house God who comes to live in the spirit of a person who has surrendered to Him.

Based on these facts and truths, that God has made the physical realm, the spirit realm and the human spirit huge and limitless in its design and purpose, and He has prepared it for us to explore, experience and learn about, I also believe that the soul of a person is also very enormous, much greater than we can fathom. But because it is not visible to the natural eye we cannot see how huge it truly is but that's another 'story' for another book.

Below you will find the reference scriptures in Luke 8: 26 – 30 concerning the man of the Gadarenes who was possessed by a legion of evil spirits.

[26] And they arrived at the country of the Gadarenes, which is over against Galilee.

[27] And when he went forth to land, there met him out of the city a certain man, which had devils long time, and ware no clothes, neither abode in any house, but in the tombs.

[28] When he saw Jesus, he cried out, and fell down before him, and with a loud voice said, What have I to do with thee, Jesus, thou Son of God most high? I beseech thee, torment me not.

[29] (For he had commanded the unclean spirit to come out of the man. For oftentimes it had caught him: and he was kept bound with chains and in

fetters; and he brake the bands, and was driven of the devil into the wilderness.)

³⁰ And Jesus asked him, saying, What is thy name? And he said, Legion: because many devils were entered into him.

³¹ And they besought him that he would not command them to go out into the deep.

³² And there was there an herd of many swine feeding on the mountain: and they besought him that he would suffer them to enter into them. And he suffered them.

³³ Then went the devils out of the man, and entered into the swine: and the herd ran violently down a steep place into the lake, and were choked.

³⁴ When they that fed them saw what was done, they fled, and went and told it in the city and in the country.

³⁵ Then they went out to see what was done; and

came to Jesus, and found the man, out of whom the devils were departed, sitting at the feet of Jesus, clothed, and in his right mind: and they were afraid.

Why is this information important for you?

It is important for you because you, I, we, have allowed things to hinder us from enjoying the benefits which God has prepared for us in these realms: Physical realm, Soul realm and the Spirit realm.

Let me reiterate: Your soul allows you to connect, communicate and interact with the physical world and the spirit world.

With my soul I have the ability to communicate, connect and interact with, not just my own body, but also with the entire physical world around me...and the physical world which is even beyond my physical reach.

But even though with my soul and its physical senses (sight, smell, taste, touch and hearing), I can and do have the ability and power to connect with the physical world, I don't see, hear, feel, taste or smell everything that exists in the physical world all at once, all at the same time.

I can only connect with the physical world that is immediately around me...within my physical sphere or reach of sight, hearing, touch, taste or smelling.

I can connect with what is beyond my physical sphere if I physically move towards it, just like I can physically connect with what is in New York if I take a plane and physically travel there.

And just like the physical realm is very huge, and I can only connect with a portion of it at a time; and be there physically in a portion of it at any given time, even so, the spiritual realm is very vast and limitless in size and I can only connect with a portion of the spiritual realm at any given time...only with that part that I spiritually move towards. And I spiritually move towards these areas of the spirit realms by focusing my attention on them.

Which means, if I want to experience having more visions and supernatural encounters I need to focus on and place more attention on it, often. And I need to do so in as much of my waking moments, as possible.

Just to recap again for emphasis and to ensure you retain what is shared:

- With my soul I have the ability to communicate, connect and interact with, not just my own spirit, but also with the entire spirit realm.

- With my soul I have the ability to connect, communicate and interact with the physical world through the 5 senses of my physical body - **Sight, Sound, Smell, Taste, and Touch**:

- With my soul I I have the ability to connect, communicate and interact with the spiritual world through the 5 senses of my spirit. My spirit being also have 5 senses like my physical body: **Sight, Sound, Smell, Taste, and Touch**...

Your Soul Is Made Up of:

A) Your mind.

Your mind consists of your thoughts and imaginations, the pictures you see and think about in your mind. It also consists of the spoken words you say inside of you (we are always speaking words, internally).

If you can **convert all those internal words you speak on the inside of you to words of praise and expressions of love for the Lord Jesus Christ,** you would experience the presence and power of God in a much greater dimension than you had known.

B) Your soul is made up of your will

Use the power of your will, to choose to always think about Him. Choose and will yourself to always obey Him and His Word, to always praise and worship Him, 24 hrs. a day, every day.

C) Your soul is made up of your Emotions

Can you allow your emotions to always desire or long for Him?

When your inner thoughts, imaginations and inner words are all focused on Him, your feelings of love and desire for Him would increase.

Your soul is already operational and always active every moment of every day, if you can direct all of or most of its energies, imaginations, inner pictures, inner words and its focus on the things of the Spirit….on the Lord Jesus Christ, the Heavenly Father and Heaven, you would begin seeing, hearing, smelling and tasting in the spirit realm, you would begin to know things supernaturally…

Then living in the realm of the spirit would become as natural and effortless as breathing is.

Chapter 3
Develop a Love-Relationship with the Lord Jesus Christ

When I was around seventeen (17) years old and seeking the Lord, I sought the Lord at that time not because I wanted something from Him. I sought Him because I genuinely wanted to love Him for who He was, and desired nothing from Him during that time when I pursued Him.

I just loved Him during those months when I search for Him, asking Him for nothing. I just loved Him during those months.

It was during that period that the Lord began to reveal Himself and His Word to me, and clearly directed and showed to me what He had called me to do for Him.

Believe it or not, that time when I had developed that Love-relationship with the Lord when I was seventeen (17) years old had sustained me for the years ahead, particularly when I had to face severe trials and tests.

How to Develop a Love-Relationship with the Lord:

How do you do that?

How do you develop a love-relationship with the Lord?

Here is how the Lord taught me to do this:

He brought to my attention what He had said in His Word where He has commanded me to love the Lord your God with all your heart, soul and **mind**…"

And thou shalt **love the Lord thy God** with all thy heart, and with all thy soul, and **with all thy mind**, and with all thy strength: this is the first commandment.

Mark 12:30   KJV

"How do I do this", I asked?

"How do I love you Lord with **ALL MY MIND**?"

"Well, since your mind think about two (2) major things daily", He shared:

- Words: Words which you speak on the inside of you.

- And images or pictures which you think in your mind, daily.

Then, it is obvious that to love the Lord with all your mind would mean that you are to use those internal words and pictures which you think daily, to love Him.

Don't waste those thoughts to think about things which are trivial, carnal, worldly, unholy, frustrating, discouraging or against His word.

He know all the thoughts you are thinking. If you are thinking love thoughts of Him, He would know it and be very pleased.

Don't you know that?

This is why when you fill your mind with love thoughts of Him and about Him, you would automatically begin to feel His presence. This is how you can feel His presence all the time, 24/7. This is how you practice the presence of the Lord.

He said in His Word, 'if you draw near to me, I will draw near to you'.

Draw near to God, and He will draw near to you…

James 4:8   KJV

When you are drawing near to Him with all your mind, with all your thoughts, with all you internal words, with all the pictures you think in your mind…He will draw near to you as He promised in His word in James 4:8

Researchers has said that we think approximately 70,000 (seventy thousand) thoughts a day (those thoughts would consist of internal words and pictures), I try with the help of the Holy Spirit to let most of those 70,000 thoughts to be love thoughts to the Lord Jesus Christ, and love-thoughts of the Lord Jesus Christ.

For instance, I use my imaginations to see and read the following sentence, repeating itself hundreds of times…using my imaginations to see it around me and filling the room or atmosphere surrounding me, written across all the sky above me, flowing in me….the words "I love you Lord Jesus with my all. I love you Yeshua with everything in me."

This is something I practice daily. This is something which I do often throughout the day, every day.

Another thing I would do to develop a love-relationship with the Lord is set a chair opposite me when I am having breakfast in the morning, and invite the Lord Jesus Christ to join me for breakfast.

I particularly do this when I am having any meal alone at home, and I have conversation with Him during that time. Telling Him how much I love Him and discussing things about His kingdom with Him, praying also for things which concerns Him.

I do not use this time to pray for personal needs or family needs.

These meal-times are all for Him, and the things which concerns Him, His will and His Kingdom.

There are other similar things which I do to help develop a love-relationship with the Lord but I have only shared two of them with you.

You can form your own love-practices to develop your relationship with the Lord; or, if you choose, you can practice the ones which I have shared with you in this book.

Behold, I stand at the door, and knock: if any man hear my voice, and open the door, **I will come in to him, and will sup with him, and he with me**.

Revelation 3:20 King James Version

Behold, I stand at the door and knock; if anyone hears *and* listens to *and* heeds My voice and opens the door, **I will come in to him and will eat with him, and he [will eat] with Me.**

Amplified Bible, Classic version

Because of Revelation 3:20 (…**I will come in to him and will eat with him, and he [will eat] with Me…**) I have breakfast and meals with the Lord Jesus Christ, daily.

And so can you.

Everything on earth and in all of creation outside of earth were all made by the Lord Jesus Christ; and all of it continues to exist by The Lord Jesus Christ. Therefore He is the most important person in all of creation; because everything was made by Him, and for Him…for His pleasure, and everything continues to exist because of Him; and without Him everything would cease to exist, instantly.

Because of this, He, **the Lord Jesus Christ, should be our main and only focus while we are living on earth.** He should be the center of our attention. We should constantly be fellowshipping, talking to and conversing with Him, every moment of every day.

Live a focused, Love Life for the Lord Jesus Christ

Develop a Love-Relationship with the Lord and you will see into the realm of the spirit. And what can help you to do this is practicing two(2) simple, yet profound things: Focus and Love.

By focusing love-thoughts on the Lord Jesus Christ, 24/7, you will eventually see in the realm of the spirit.

"How long I have to do this practice before I see in the realm of the spirit?" You may ask.

That I do not know. I never checked to see how long it took me before I saw in the sprit realm after practicing a focused, love-life with the Lord. Because that was never my objective when I first started practicing these things. It was never because I wanted to see in the spirit realm. It was and still is because I wanted to just love Him more and more for who He is and what He has done for me; and because I wanted to get to know Him in a much deeper way. I wanted to truly experience practically what it means to be one with Him….One with Him in word, thought and deed.

How can you focus Love-Thoughts on the Lord Jesus Christ every moment of every day?

There are ways you can do this. I will share them with you, things which the Lord had taught me.

In Matthew 5 the Lord Jesus Christ said if you look upon a woman to lust after her in your heart you have already committed adultery…also, if you think thoughts of hate towards someone in your mind, you have already committed murder in your heart.

The Lord Jesus Christ is sharing with us a spiritual law here: If you do anything in your imaginations good or bad, it is considered as if it had actually been done in the physical realm in the eyes of God.

Imaginations = Reality in the spirit realm

What you focus on the inside of you, in your imaginations, is considered by God, as if you are actually doing the things you are focusing on in the eyesight of Almighty God. I am specifically talking about the deeds of the flesh and the things of the spirit.

Here is an example of what I mean:

- If you focus or see yourself in the garden of heaven eating a large, luscious strawberry from a tree there…taking a bite into this lovely, sweet fruit – In God's mind and eyes you are actually doing it. You are actually there partaking of that fruit. You cannot claim or brush it off as that is just my imaginations and it doesn't matter. It does matter with God. And isn't He the one that you are trying to please, not yourself? If He is pleased that should settle it.

- Secondly, if you use your imaginations to focus on seeing yourself before the throne of Almighty God with the Lord Jesus Christ sitting on His right hand…if you see yourself there in your imaginations, telling the Lord Jesus Christ, these words "I love you Lord Jesus." In the Lord's eyes, you are actually there doing so. It is not a figment of your imagination and doesn't matter with Him. It does matter with Him. All those thoughts are actually recorded in special books in heaven.

Those are just a couple ways I use my imaginations to love Him.

Of course, I have more love-practices which I implement to develop my relationship with the Lord.

Therefore, if you want to see in the spirit realm, you can do so all the time by simply using your imaginations (your thoughts and inner words) to see yourself in heaven participating in worship with the saints and angels there, or before the throne of God praising Him, or simply walking around in heaven experiencing and witnessing the beauty there. If you practice this, heaven will always be close to you, you will be living in and experiencing the joys and beauties of heaven all the time, every day.

I am speaking about having and maintaining this internal posture all the time, every day - seeing yourself before His throne, before His presence, speaking and listening to Him.

Isn't this how you develop first-love with someone?

- By spending quality time with them
- By always thinking about them. In fact, they are actually on your mind for almost the entire day.
- By thinking about what you are going to do for them.
- By calling them on the phone and spending hours talking to them almost every day, or every day.
- By spending alone times with that person, often.
- By including them in some of your daily. Activities. Activities like shopping, having a meal together, cooking, cleaning, washing clothes, feeding the poor, visiting the sick…etc.

Signs you are not focused on Him:

- ✓ If you are focused on the faults of others you are not focused on Him. It means you have taken your eyes off of Him to turn and look at others.

- ✓ If you are thinking and talking about your problems you are not focused on Him. It means you have taken your eyes off of seeing yourself before His throne, before His presence, speaking and listening to Him, and you have turned them to look at and talk about your problems.

- ✓ If you are jealous or envious of others.

- ✓ If you are focused on the things you don't have, and which others possess.

- ✓ If you are thinking less of yourself th7an the word of God says about you.

- ✓ If you get angry at others because they did not do what you wanted them to do or not do; or they did not say to you things you wanted them to say to you.

The Lord Jesus Christ and heaven seem very far from you because you are not practicing this: Focus and Love….Use your focus (your thoughts, imaginations, inner words…) to love Him throughout the day. You can do so right now. **Take your focus off of you, others, the world, and focus them entirely on Him.**

The major purpose of this exercise is to stir up your spirit within you to connect with and experience the spirit realm – To become one with the Lord Jesus Christ.

If you practice this exercise often, it would not be long before you start to actually see in the spirit realm in dreams, trances, and visions.

"You can't work your way into an experience with Me, but you can love your way into one." I heard those words when I was walking and praying in my prayer room. 5/6/2021, around 12.00 noon.

I end this chapter by advising you to love your way into experiences with Him.

Chapter 4
Be Still – practice being still

Another proven way through which you can see in the spirit realm is by being totally still, physically and mentally, for at least one hour or more, or until the realm of the spirit opens up to you.

Be still, and know that I am God: I will be exalted among the heathen, I will be exalted in the earth.

Psalms 46:10 KJV

Isaiah 30:15 For thus says the Lord God, the Holy One of Israel: "In returning and rest you shall be saved; In **quietness and confidence** shall be your strength."

When a person is in a coma, their physical senses are suspended (according to those who had been in a coma and recovered), particularly the senses they need to communicate with in this physical world around us. But although their body is in this temporary form of suspension, their spirit is still alive and active, and the spiritual senses of their spirit can still see, hear, smell, feel and know what is happening in the physical and spiritual worlds around them.

So while their 5 (five) physical senses are in suspension, their spirit man takes over, and they become more connected to and in touch with the spirit realm.

This is also why the scriptures encourages us to become still before the Lord. It says to 'Be still, and know that I am God...'

If you practice for a specific amount of time each day to be totally STILL physically and mentally, you will experience the dimensions of the spirit realm.

Being totally STILL, physically and mentally have been known to be an exercise which leads to your spiritual senses becoming more alert, active and dominant. where you begin to see, hear, feel and touch the spirit realm, where you begin to know things supernaturally. **Because it mimics an experience similar to when a person**

is in a coma or a trance....an experience where their physical senses are suspended, and the spirit man takes over.

How do I do this?

How can I be totally still inwardly and outwardly?

Here's how:

1. Find a quiet place in your home or somewhere else convenient to you, where you won't be disturbed.

2. Sit quietly in a chair in a relaxed position. I personally sit in a computer chair with my head resting on the headrest or back of the chair. Make sure it is comfortable for your head in the event you have to stay in that position for 30 minutes or more, or else the back of your head could start to hurt you after a while.

3. Next, close your eyes to shut out the outer, physical world.

4. If need be, you can also put ear plugs in your ears to block out the outside noises - Noises which could cause you to lose focus.

Please, don't carry your phone or any communication devices with you during this period, or have the computer on at this time. You would more than likely get distracted by it, if you do.

5. You can then focus on the darkness you see at the back of your eyelids when you close your eyes. And stay focused on this until you begin to see into the spirit realm. The time it takes for the spirit realm to open up will vary with everyone. But normally, it takes approximately 45 minutes of total stillness – being physically still (not moving at all) and

not thinking of anything except focusing on the darkness you will see when you close your eyes.

Or, if you choose to keep your eyes open, you can focus on a blank wall before you, without thinking about anything or moving your physical body in any way. Just total stillness for at least 45 minutes or more.

This is a practice which many (including myself) has testified, works. It opens up the spirit realm to you. It opens your spiritual eyes to the spirit realm.

6. Please note, it will take constant, patient and continuous practice to achieve this. Initially, you may not make 5 or 10 minutes before you lose your still position, physically and mentally. But keep practicing until you can reach up to 45 minutes or more being totally still. It may take you a week, couple of weeks

or more to achieve this, but don't give up. Be persistent and relentless in this practice.

7. At first, you may begin to see clear images or quick flashes of images before you. Some may make sense, others may not make sense. Either way, just allow the process to transpire for as long as possible. The more you do this is the more the spirit realm will begin to open up to you, to the point where you can openly see in the spirit realm with your physical eyes opened.

What should I do today?

Practice being totally still mentally and physically for 15 minutes, then 30 minutes, then 1 hour and more (not thinking about anything during this set-apart time)

Chapter 5

Instant and Complete Obedience – obedience opens the door to the Supernatural

Total obedience to the revealed will of God, and complete obedience to the Rhema Word of God are also spiritual door-openers to the unseen realm.

This is another path you can take to see in the spirit realm. It is to do the opposite actions which Adam and Eve took in Genesis 3 verse 7 '…**and the eyes of them both were opened**…'

This happened when they ate of the fruit of the tree of the knowledge of good and evil.

Read it for yourself in Genesis 3: 1 – 7 King James Version

3 Now the serpent was more crafty than any of the wild animals the LORD God had made. He said to the woman, "Did God really say, 'You must not eat from any tree in the garden'?"

² The woman said to the serpent, "We may eat fruit from the trees in the garden, ³ but God did say, 'You must not eat fruit from the tree that is in the middle of the garden, and you must not touch it, or you will die.'"

⁴ "You will not certainly die," the serpent said to the woman. ⁵ "For God knows that when you eat from it your eyes will be opened, and you will be like God, knowing good and evil."

⁶ When the woman saw that the fruit of the tree was good for food and pleasing to the eye, and also desirable for gaining wisdom, she took some and ate it. She also gave some to her husband, who was with her, and he ate it.

⁷ **Then the eyes of both of them were opened**, and they realized they were naked; so they sewed fig leaves together and made coverings for themselves.

When Adam and Eve disobeyed God in the Garden of Eden they were able to see and know things in the physical realm which were hidden from them, from their knowledge and physical sight.

The moment they disobeyed God they were able to see and know things in the natural realm which were unknown to them prior to sin.

The opposite is also true if you want to see in the spirit realm, particularly the heavenly spiritual realm.

Do the opposite actions they took and you will see in the realm of the spirit.

Their eyes were opened to the physical world when they ate the fruit which God told them not to eat of…similarly when you partake of the Word of God, and fully obey Him with your whole heart, your eyes would be opened to see God just like they did in the Garden of Eden before they sinned.

> A. If you obey God's revealed will found in the Holy Bible, consistently, every day, your spiritual eyes and knowledge would be opened to see and know things supernaturally in the spiritual realm. That is, the things which

He has already instructed us to do in His Word the Holy Bible.

God's revealed will is found in His Word, the Holy Bible....By consistently obeying whatever He instructed us in His Word to do, He would open up the realm of the spirit to us.

   B. If you obey the Rhema Word of God, that is, the things He asks you to do for Him through the voice of His Holy Spirit who resides inside you. When you obey Him like this your spiritual eyes and ears would be opened to see and hear in the spirit realm.

By being totally obedient to Him and His word – His Logos and Rhema Words, your spiritual eyes would be opened.

There are two (2) Greek words used in scripture to describe the Word of God:

One is 'Logos', which refers to the written Word of God, the Holy Bible. And the other is 'Rhema', the spoken Word of God, which the Holy Spirit speaks on the inside of you every day.

The 'Logos' Word of God in our day would be The Holy Bible.

Included in the Holy Bible are instructions and commandments which the Heavenly Father commands us to listen and adhere to, and to keep and obey.

The Rhema word of God is that still small voice you hear on the inside of you instructing, guiding and telling you (by His Holy Spirit) what you should do and what you should not do.

Every day we hear the Rhema word of God.

Let me give you an example of the 'Rhema' Word of God, though.

Many years ago, the Lord had told me not to purchase a certain used car I was intent on purchasing. I heard that word plainly on the inside of me. But I did not obey that Rhema word from the Lord. As a result, that car which I purchased only worked well for about a month. After that, I was practically by the mechanic shop almost every month, having to fix one thing or another in that vehicle. I ended up spending more money in repairs for that car than I paid for it.

This is how important it is to hear and obey those Rhema words from God which we all receive daily, whether we listen to it or ignore it.

This is an example of The Rhema Word of God.

It is not written in The Holy Bible that I should not purchase that vehicle which I bought at that time, but while in prayer, I received this instruction from Him for me not to do so. But I disobeyed and paid a significant price for that disobedience, for not obeying that Rhema word of God. And so will you if you don't hear and obey those Rhema words from God which we all receive daily.

Please remember Partial obedience is disobedience.

If you walk in full obedience to Him, His Rhema words to you, and to His commandments in the Holy

Bible, totally obeying the things He asks you to do for Him through the voice of His Holy Spirit on the inside of you, then you too, would see and hear in the spirit realm very clearly and with much details.

In the past, I too, had ignored His Rhema words several times in my life and had lived to regret those moments. If I had only obeyed His Rhema words to me during each of those times I would have saved myself from lots of heartaches, sorrows and loss…heavy financial loss, obligations and preventable debts to name a few.

John 14:21-23
Amplified Bible, Classic Edition

[21] The person who has My commands and keeps them is the one who [really] loves Me; and whoever [really] loves Me will be loved by My Father, and **I [too] will love him and will show (reveal, manifest) Myself to him. I will let Myself be clearly seen by him** and make Myself real to him.

The Lord Jesus Christ has promised that if you obey Him and keep His commandments, He will show, reveal, and manifest Himself to you. And **He will allow Himself to be clearly seen by you.**

Do you want to clearly see Him?

Here are the conditions for those encounters:

a. Love Him with your all.

b. Keep His Commandments – Obey His Logos Word, the things He has commanded us to do in His Word, the Holy Bible.

c. Obey His Rhema words – quickly do what He tells you to do through the inner voice of His Holy Spirit. Even if it means sitting next to a beggar on the street and talking with him…sharing your food, money and Christ with that person.

When you meet the above conditions, He will fulfill His part of the agreement found in John 14: 21 -23

The Lord Jesus Christ has promised in John 14: 21 – 23 that if you obey Him and keep His commandments, He will show, reveal, and manifest Himself to you. And **He will allow Himself to be clearly seen by you.**

You will clearly see Him.

Chapter 6

Love not the World

Don't love the world's ways. Don't love the world's goods. Love of the world squeezes out love for the Father. Practically everything that goes on in the world—wanting your own way, wanting everything for yourself, wanting to appear important—has nothing to do with the Father. It just isolates you from Him. The world and all its wanting, wanting, wanting is on the way out—but whoever does what God wants is set for eternity.

1 John 2: 16, The Message Bible Translation

Here is the King James Version of 1 John 2:15 – 17

[15] Love not the world, neither the things that are in the world. If any man love the world, the love of the Father is not in him.

[16] For all that is in the world, the **lust of the flesh**, and the **lust of the eyes**, and the **pride of life**, is

not of the Father, but is of the world.

¹⁷ And the world passeth away, and the lust thereof: but he that doeth the will of God abideth for ever.

What is the lust of the flesh?

What is the lust of the eyes?

What is the pride of life?

The lust of the flesh:

The lust of the flesh can be clearly seen in the book of Galatians 5: 16 - 21

¹⁶ This I say then, **Walk in the Spirit**, and ye shall not fulfil the **lust of the flesh**.

¹⁷ For the flesh lusteth against the Spirit, and the Spirit against the flesh: and these are contrary the one to the other: so that ye cannot do the things that ye would.

¹⁸ But if ye be led of the Spirit, ye are not under the

law.

¹⁹ Now the works of the flesh are manifest, which are these; Adultery, fornication, uncleanness, lasciviousness,

²⁰ Idolatry, witchcraft, hatred, variance, emulations, wrath, strife, seditions, heresies,

²¹ Envyings, murders, drunkenness, revellings, and such like: of the which I tell you before, as I have also told you in time past, that they which do such things shall not inherit the kingdom of God.

This is the Amplified Translation of Galations 5: 16 – 21

¹⁶ But I say, walk *and* live [habitually] in the [Holy] Spirit [responsive to *and* controlled *and* guided by the Spirit]; then you will certainly not gratify the cravings *and* desires of the flesh (of human nature without God).

¹⁷ For the desires of the flesh are opposed to the [Holy] Spirit, and the [desires of the] Spirit are opposed to the flesh (godless human nature); for these are antagonistic to each other [continually withstanding and in conflict with each other], so that you are not free *but* are prevented from doing what you desire to do.

¹⁸ But if you are guided (led) by the [Holy] Spirit, you are not subject to the Law.

¹⁹ Now the doings (practices) of the flesh are clear (obvious): they are immorality, impurity, indecency,

²⁰ Idolatry, sorcery, enmity, strife, jealousy, anger (ill temper), selfishness, divisions (dissensions), party spirit (factions, sects with peculiar opinions, heresies),

²¹ Envy, drunkenness, carousing, and the like. I warn you beforehand, just as I did previously, that those who do such things shall not inherit the kingdom of God.

These three (3) things: The lust of the flesh, the lust of the eyes and the pride of life are enemies to seeing in the spirit, they close our eyes to the spirit realm.

These are Some Signs of the Lust of the Flesh:

- ✓ Adultery – being married and having sex with another person other than your wife or husband. A married person can also commit adultery in their heart by secretly desiring or imagining being with someone who is not their spouse.

- ✓ Fornication – having sex outside of marriage. Being single or engaged and partaking of sex. Participating in oral sex, masturbation, pornography, and other illicit sexual activities

- ✓ Uncleanness

- ✓ Lasciviousness – unbridled lust

- ✓ Idolatry – worshipping idols. This goes beyond the worship of just a physical image - believers have also made idols of money, their job, their car, their home, etc.

- ✓ Witchcraft

- ✓ Hatred

- ✓ Variance – mean spirit

- ✓ Emulations - is the translation of the Greek word zelos ("zeal," "earnestness," "enthusiasm") where it is classed among "the works of the flesh" and **signifies the stirring up of jealousy or envy in others, because of what we are, or have, or profess**. https://www.biblestudytools.com/encyclopedias/isbe/emulation.html

- ✓ Wrath – outbursts of anger.

- ✓ Strife - Strife refers to the stirring up of discord and division.

- ✓ Seditions - Sedition often includes **subversion of a constitution and incitement of discontent toward, or insurrection against established authority**. https://en.wikipedia.org/wiki/Sedition

- ✓ Heresies - Heresies signify self-chosen doctrines not emanating from God. **Easton's Bible Dictionary**

- ✓ Envying

- ✓ Murders – please remember it was the Lord Jesus who said that if you hate someone you have committed murder in your heart. The Lord considers this as murder.

- ✓ Drunkenness

- ✓ Reveling – comes from the Greek word 'komos' which means letting loose, rioting.

…and such like:

What is the Lust of the eyes?

The lust of the eyes can be described as the sinful, craving desire to want to have the things we see, such as money, material possessions, houses, cars, a certain physical appearance, or even looking at someone lustfully. Our eyes see everything physical around us and our own eyes can cause us to covet or want something we do not possess.

As an example, Eve committed the sinful desire of the lust of the eyes when she saw the forbidden fruit and lusted after it. The Bible tells us, "When the woman saw that the fruit of the tree was good for food and pleasing to the eye, and also desirable for gaining wisdom, she took some and ate it. She also gave some to her husband, who was with her, and he ate it" (**Genesis 3:6**).

https://www.christianity.com/wiki/bible/why-does-the-lust-of-the-eyes-come-from-the-world.html

What is the pride of Life?

The pride of life is having an attitude that credits all that is accomplished in your life to your own abilities, to your own strength, to your own knowledge….instead of attributing all which had been accomplished in your life to the Lord Jesus Christ.

Pride goes before destruction and a haughty spirit before a fall.

Proverbs 16:18   KJV

For all that is in the world, the lust of the flesh, and the lust of the eyes, and the pride of life, is not of the Father, but is of the world.

1 John 2:16   KJV

The lust of the flesh, the lust of the eyes and the pride of life is all wrapped up in one word:

Self….Me, myself and I.

It is thinking, and saying or doing things which primarily focuses on yourself without any concern for how it will or may negatively impact upon the Lord or others.

Self is the opposite of God's love – Agape Love. If you walk, live, think, talk and do things with Agape Love (God kind of Love) being the guiding and motivating force behind it all, then you would be walking and living In the Spirit. Then you would be abiding in Him, and He in you.

On the 27-03-2021 the Lord revealed to me that **it is 'Focus' which makes and keeps the flesh alive.** It is focus which ensures that the lust of the flesh, the lust of the eyes and the pride of life is alive and kept alive. **And it is also focus which can subdue the flesh and render it inactive**.

It is the cares of this life and the deceitfulness of riches…the lust of the eyes, the lust of the flesh and the pride of life which keeps our spiritual eyes and ears closed.

One simple way to overcome the lust of the eyes, the lust of the flesh and the pride of life is to pray in tongues every moment of every day, before, during and after we face these three (3) opponents of the spirit. If we practice this, then the spirit would easily have victory over the flesh.

It is these three (3) opponents which keep the flesh alive and keep veils before our spiritual eyes: the lust of the flesh, the lust of the eyes and the pride of life – they are the ones which keep us from seeing in the spirit.

If we change our focus and maintain that change of focus on the Lord Jesus Christ, then these fleshly opponents will be subdued and die almost instantly. **Then, you would begin to experience activity in your spiritual senses.**

However, like the apostle Paul, we would have to die daily – we would have **to maintain a daily death to the flesh**…to these three (3) barriers in order to experience and keep on experiencing a total opening and activating of our spiritual senses.

Remember though, once we are in this life, these three (3) opponents would constantly try to be resurrected day in and day out. So stay vigilant.

If we do die daily to those three (3) barriers, Then we would begin seeing in the spirit realm very easily. We would begin having all our spiritual senses activated. The spiritual veils would be removed.

The cure for these three (3) opponents: The lust of the flesh, the lust of the eyes and the pride of life is the fruit of the Spirit.

But **the fruit of the Spirit** is love, joy, peace, longsuffering, gentleness, goodness, faith, Meekness, temperance: against such **the**re is no law.

Galatians 5: 22, 23   KJV

Chapter 7

Live a Sinless Life

If I don't sin, if I live a sinless life - I will see Him.

Sin is a selfish act. It is thinking of yourself. It is satisfying your selfish desires.

If you are solely thinking of pleasing the Lord Jesus Christ in everything that you say, think and do because you love Him dearly, you will not sin when you are tempted to sin.

Your Sins Have Hid His Face from You

Isaiah 59:1, 2 King James Version

59 Behold, the LORD's hand is not shortened, that it cannot save; neither his ear heavy that it cannot hear:

2 But your iniquities have separated between you and your God, and **your sins have hid his face**

from you, that he will not hear.

Ezekiel 39:23   KJV

And the heathen shall know that the house of Israel went into captivity for their iniquity: because they trespassed against me, therefore **hid I my face** from them, and gave them into the hand of their enemies: so fell they all by the sword.

Ezekiel 39:24   KJV

According to their uncleanness and according to their transgressions have I done unto them, and hid my face from them.

Deuteronomy 31:18   KJV

And I will surely **hide my face** in that day for all the evils which they shall have wrought, in that they are turned unto other gods.

Isaiah 33:14 – 17   KJV

[14] The sinners in Zion are afraid; fearfulness hath surprised the hypocrites. Who among us shall dwell

with the devouring fire**? who among us shall dwell with everlasting burnings?**

¹⁵ He that walketh righteously, and speaketh uprightly; he that despiseth the gain of oppressions, that shaketh his hands from holding of bribes, that stoppeth his ears from hearing of blood, and shutteth his eyes from seeing evil;

¹⁶ He shall dwell on high: his place of defence shall be the munitions of rocks: bread shall be given him; his waters shall be sure.

¹⁷ Thine eyes shall see the king in his beauty: they shall behold the land that is very far off.

If sin separates a person from God, and **causes God to hide His face from that individual**, then the opposite is also true, a person who does not have sin will be connected to God, and God will reveal His face to that person.

God will reveal Himself, His face, to the person who

does not have sin in his or her life.

The Lord Jesus Christ would reveal Himself to the person who is not living in sin…to the person who is living a sinless life every minute, every hour, every day, every week, every month, every year and every moment. This person would have open and ready access to the spirit realm and heaven, daily.

When you receive the Lord Jesus Christ into your heart as your Lord and Saviour, He cleanses you from all sin and delivers you from the power and control of sin.

What that means is: You don't have to sin once you have the Lord Jesus Christ living in your heart or spirit.

You can now live a sinless life. He has given you the power to live sin-free or sinless.

I will say that again, "You don't have to sin. Once Jesus lives in your heart, sin no longer have any control or power over you, and you don't have to yield to its bidding."

But if you do sin, He has already provided a means for you to be forgiven of that sin and be instantly restored to a clean, sinless state.

Now though this is true, it is not a license for you to intentionally and willfully sin and then seek God for forgiveness.

1 John 1:7   King James Version

But if we walk in the light, as He is in the light, we have fellowship one with another, and the blood of Jesus Christ His Son cleanseth us from all sin.

1 John 2:1- 2 King James Version

1. My little children, these things write I unto you, that ye sin not. And if any man sin, we have an advocate with the Father, Jesus Christ the righteous:

2. And he is the propitiation for our sins: and not for ours only, but also for the sins of the whole world.

How can I stop sinning?

How can I not sin?

This is how we don't sin:

If I abide in Him, I will not sin, and I will know Him.

⁶ Whosoever abideth in him sinneth not: whosoever sinneth hath not seen him, neither known him.
1 John 3: 6   KJV

Whosoever is born of God doth not commit sin; for His seed remaineth in Him: **and He cannot sin**, because He is born of God.

1 John 3: 9   KJV

My friend, you do not have to commit sin or live in sin. The Lord plainly states that in 1 John 3: 9 (see previous scripture verse).

1John 3: 2 - 9

² Beloved, now are we the sons of God, and it doth not yet appear what we shall be: but we know that,

when He shall appear, we shall be like Him; for we shall see Him as He is.

³ And every man that hath this hope in him purifieth himself, even as He is pure.

⁴ Whosoever committeth sin transgresseth also the law: for sin is the transgression of the law.

⁵ And ye know that He was manifested to take away our sins; and in Him is no sin.

⁶ Whosoever abideth in Him sinneth not: whosoever sinneth hath not seen Him, neither known Him.

⁷ Little children, let no man deceive you: he that doeth righteousness is righteous, even as He is righteous.

⁸ He that committeth sin is of the devil; for the devil sinneth from the beginning. For this purpose the Son of God was manifested, that He might destroy the works of the devil.

[9] **Whosoever is born of God doth not commit sin**; for His seed remaineth in him: **and he cannot sin**, because he is born of God.

Abide in Him

John 15:4

Abide in me, and I in you. As the branch cannot bear fruit of itself, except it **abide in** the vine; no more can ye, except ye **abide in** me.

John 15:5

I am the vine, ye are the branches: He that **abide**th **in** me, and I **in** him, the same bringeth forth much fruit: for without me ye can do nothing.

John 15:6

If a man **abide** not **in** me, he is cast forth as a branch, and is withered; and men gather them, and cast them **in**to the fire, and they are burned.

John 15:7

If ye **abide in** me, and my words **abide in** you, ye shall ask what ye will, and it shall be done unto you.

John 15:10

If ye keep my commandments, ye shall **abide in** my love; even as I have kept my Father's commandments, and **abide in** his love.

1 John 2:6   KJV

He that saith he **abide**th **in** Him ought himself also so to walk, even as He walked.

1 John 2:10   KJV

He that loveth his brother **abide**th **in** the light, and there is none occasion of stumbling **in** him.

1 John 2:28   KJV

And now, little children, **abide in** Him; that, when He shall appear, we may have confidence, and not be ashamed before Him at His coming.

1 John 3:6   KJV

Whosoever abideth in Him sinneth not: whosoever sinneth hath not seen Him, neither known Him.

1 John 3:14   KJV

We know that we have passed from death unto life, because we love the brethren. He that loveth not his brother **abide**th **in** death.

1 John 3:24   KJV

And he that keepeth His commandments dwelleth **in** Him, and He **in** him. And hereby we know that He **abide**th **in** us, by the Spirit which He hath given us.

2 John 1:9   KJV

Whosoever transgresseth, and **abide**th not **in** the doctrine of Christ, hath not God. He that **abide**th **in** the doctrine of Christ, he hath both the Father and the Son.

How do I do this?

How do I abide in Him so that I would not live in sin....so that I can live a sinless life?

What do I have to do to abide in Him?

The word 'abide' means to remain, stay, live, lodge, make your home in....

John 15: 4, 5 Amplified Bible Translation, Classic

[4] Dwell in Me, and I will dwell in you. [Live in Me, and I will live in you.] Just as no branch can bear fruit of itself without abiding in (being vitally united to) the vine, neither can you bear fruit unless you abide in Me.

[5] I am the Vine; you are the branches. Whoever lives in Me and I in him bears much (abundant) fruit. However, apart from Me [cut off from vital union with Me] you can do nothing.

Here is how you abide in Him:

- By opening the door of your heart and receiving Him into your life as Lord and Saviour.

[20] Behold, I stand at the door and knock; if anyone hears *and* listens to *and* heeds My voice and opens the door, I will come in to him and will eat with him, and he [will eat] with Me. Revelation 3:20 Amplified Bible

- By having His Holy Spirit dwelling in you

- By spending much time with Him in prayer…not asking Him for anything, but simply spending quality time with Him telling Him how much you love Him. By living very close to Him in prayer. By developing a love-relationship with Him.

- By not sinning

- By having His Word living in you. By being full of His Word. And by being refilled with His Word, daily.

- By obeying His commandments

- By loving others

- By walking as Jesus walked

Practice including the Lord Jesus Christ in all you think, say and do…in all your activities throughout the day.

For example:

Let's say I have to go to the grocery to buy some groceries, I may say to the Lord,

"Dearest Jesus, I have to go to the grocery to buy some groceries, I ask that you would join me. I ask that you would go with me to the grocery to shop for these items, Lord."

Or, if I have to cook or bake,

I may say, "Lord Jesus, I ask that you help me to cook and bake today, Lord. Let's make excellent lunch and dessert together."

Why don't you do the same, today, right now?

Include Him in all your activities today.

Don't you know He knows all the thoughts you are thinking throughout the day?...And if you are talking to Him and asking Him to join you in all your activities He would hear and answer your sincere prayers?

Please note, He will only join you in activities that are not wrong to do.

I ask Him every day to help me cook and bake excellent meals; or go to the grocery with me....and to join and help me to do a host of other things which I do daily.

I know you may already know this, but you won't believe there are some people who would actually need to hear me say this.

What are the benefits of abiding in Him?

- Seeing the Lord Jesus Christ and the Heavenly Father

- Bearing much fruit

- Asking in prayer for what you will and having Him give it to you

If you practice abiding in Him you would not sin. But if you sin you can ask Him for forgiveness and He will forgive you of your sin/s and cleanse you from all unrighteousness.

Romans 6:2   KJV

God forbid. How shall we, that are **dead to** sin, live any longer therein?

Romans 6:11   KJV

Likewise reckon ye also yourselves **to** be **dead** indeed unto sin, but alive unto God through Jesus Christ our Lord.

1 Peter 2:24   KJV

Who his own self bare our sins in His own body on the tree, that we, being **dead to** sins, should live unto righteousness: by whose stripes ye were healed.

We are not sinners saved by grace.

We were sinners, but we are now cleansed, set free and delivered from sin and its power and control by the grace of God and the blood of the Lord Jesus Christ.

This is a major difference to the theology which had been taught to the believers in Christ, that we are sinners saved by grace.

If you live a sinless life daily, you will see His face, no buts, ifs or maybe. He promises that you will if you live a life without sin.

Ezekiel 22:26   KJV

Her priests have violated my law, and have profaned mine holy things: they have put no

difference between the holy and profane, neither have they shewed difference between the unclean and the clean, and have hid their eyes from my Sabbaths, and I am profaned among them.

Ezekiel 44:23 KJV

And they shall teach my people the difference between the holy and profane, and cause them to discern between the unclean and the clean.

Leviticus 11:44 KJV

For I am the LORD your God: **ye** shall therefore sanctify yourselves, and ye shall **be holy**; **for I am holy**: neither shall **ye** defile yourselves with any manner of creeping thing that creepeth upon the earth.

Leviticus 11:45. KJV

For I am the LORD that bringeth you up out of the land of Egypt, to **be** your God: **ye** shall therefore be ye holy for I am holy.

Leviticus 20:26 KJV

And ye shall be holy unto me: for I the LORD am holy, and have severed you from other people, that ye should be mine.

1 Peter 1:16   KJV

Because it is written, **Be ye holy; for I am holy**.

Holiness opens the doors to the spiritual realm. Living a sinless life activates your spiritual senses.

Chapter 8

Fasting & Prayer

What is Fasting and Prayer?

The Biblical concept of Fasting and Prayer is setting aside a specific period of time to seek the Lord in prayer and the study of His word without eating any form of food.

Fasting and Prayer does open up your eyes and spiritual senses to the spirit realm, particularly long periods of Prayer and Fasting.

One of the ways you can see in the spirit realm is through Fasting and praying, usually long periods of fasting and praying - 40 days and more, till the spirit realm opens up to you.

This kind of fasting and praying opens your spiritual eyes to see in the spirit realm.

Many believers have experienced seeing in the spirit realm when they do long periods of fasting and praying.

I myself have experienced this.

For me personally, my spiritual senses became more active when I had fasted and prayed continuously for 175 days.

I did not plan to fast that long, but I just felt an urge to fast, and just continued to fast for that length of time. It was not something preplanned or pre-determined.

At that time heavy witchcraft was being practiced and launched against me in the area I lived in, and I felt the need to counteract it with much fasting and prayer. I prayed throughout the day, but particularly in the early morning hours between 12 midnight to 5.30 a.m.

…That was a partial fast.

During that time I fasted for at least 12 – 18 hours a day.

I stayed away from all food during that period and only drank a little water for those days.

I cannot recall how soon or what day during that fast when my spiritual senses became more alert and active, but I do know that I had open visions, trances, 100 percent accurate dreams, revelations, and heightened spiritual perceptions; and those experiences continued to be active every day till present.

Since then I have had and continue to have supernatural experiences, daily.

Here are just a couple experiences He has allowed me to have:

- The Lord Jesus Christ had taken me on the 25-02-2021 (before it happened), to see a ship that was stuck in the Suez Canal for 6 days. I saw the name written on the side of the ship. From the size of the ship and its colour, I knew it was a cargo ship. I stood there with Him watching this event transpire. This event literally took place on the 23rd March 2021, approximately one month after the Lord had showed it to me. The Lord allowed me to see the event before it happened.

- The Lord Jesus had also shown me the Covid. 19 pandemic and the shutdown of the world about 3 – 4 weeks before it happened.

- The Lord Jesus had also shown me before it happened, the huge Starship rocket that Elon Musk had designed and launched recently. It felt intimidating when I saw it. I never knew that he was working on a rocket because I was not following up on his latest exploits.

- At another time, The Lord Jesus had carried me to the doorway of a huge underground system. There was a lady sitting on a chair just outside the door. She handed the Lord and myself a cleaning tool. We then entered this huge underground tunnel and after we walked for a short while inside there, I asked Him what this place was. He said we were below a children's home for girls, and we were there to do some cleanup. The children there were being abused. This place was in Europe, but I don't know exactly which European country it was.

Fasting and Prayer is an integral part of my life. I fast and pray often. And the Lord Jesus in His grace allows me to continue to have these kinds of spiritual experiences, every day.

You do not have to fast 175 days like I did, but you can fast as many days as you feel impressed to do, to have your spiritual senses activated.

The Partial Fast is not the only kind of fast you can embark on, **there are different kinds of fasts** which were practiced throughout history, and which are spoken about in the Holy Bible.

I have listed some of the kinds of fasts which are practiced today.

1. **Partial Fast**

   There are different types of Partial Fasts – I only mentioned 2 types below.

A. The Night Fast: This is a partial fast of 12 hours from 6 p.m. to 6 a.m. – from sundown to sunup,

   In the book of Daniel, after King Darius was tricked into passing a law which caused Daniel to be cast into a lion's den, he (the king) passed the night fasting without food, sleep, entertainment, music, etc. after Daniel was set up by jealous rulers in the reign of the Persian Empire and cast into the lion's den.

Daniel 6: 16 – 19

   [16] Then the king commanded, and they brought Daniel, and cast him into the den of lions. Now the king spake and said unto Daniel, Thy God whom thou servest continually, he will deliver thee.

¹⁷ And a stone was brought, and laid upon the mouth of the den; and the king sealed it with his own signet, and with the signet of his lords; that the purpose might not be changed concerning Daniel.

¹⁸ **Then the king went to his palace, and passed the night fasting**: neither were instruments of musick brought before him: and his sleep went from him.

¹⁹ Then the king arose very early in the morning, and went in haste unto the den of lions.

You can switch up these hours if you choose. You can go from 6 a.m. to 6 p.m. instead. You can do a daytime partial fast if that suits you better than the night fast.

B. **The second kind of Partial Fast is the Daniel Fast**

This type of fast consist of eating in moderation, only fruits, vegetables and whole grains, and the only drink used for this fast is water.

Daniel fasted this type of partial fast with prayer for 3 full weeks, 21 days.

Was this fast effective?

Oh yes! Very effective.

He had 100 percent accurate dreams, visions and revelations during that time.

In fact, his 21 days of fasting and prayer caused God to release angels from heaven to bring revelations and visions of the future and understanding of the plans of God.

His fasting and praying also resulted in angelic war in the second heaven between the angels of God and the rulers of darkness which were presiding over that region.

Daniel 10: 1 – 10 King James Version

10. In the third year of Cyrus king of Persia a thing

was revealed unto Daniel, whose name was called Belteshazzar; and the thing was true, but the time appointed was long: and he understood the thing, and had understanding of the vision.

² In those days I Daniel was mourning three full weeks.

³ I ate no pleasant bread, neither came flesh nor wine in my mouth, neither did I anoint myself at all, till three whole weeks were fulfilled.

⁴ And in the four and twentieth day of the first month, as I was by the side of the great river, which is Hiddekel;

⁵ Then I lifted up mine eyes, and looked, and behold a certain man clothed in linen, whose loins were girded with fine gold of Uphaz:

⁶ His body also was like the beryl, and his face as the appearance of lightning, and his eyes as lamps of fire, and his arms and his feet like in colour to

polished brass, and the voice of his words like the voice of a multitude.

⁷ And I Daniel alone saw the vision: for the men that were with me saw not the vision; but a great quaking fell upon them, so that they fled to hide themselves.

⁸ Therefore I was left alone, and saw this great vision, and there remained no strength in me: for my comeliness was turned in me into corruption, and I retained no strength.

⁹ Yet heard I the voice of his words: and when I heard the voice of his words, then was I in a deep sleep on my face, and my face toward the ground.

¹⁰ And, behold, a hand touched me, which set me upon my knees and upon the palms of my hands.

2. **24 Hour Water Fasts** – From 1 to 40 consecutive days or more.

A 24-Hour Water Fast is a fast in which you eat nothing for 24 hours. You only drink water during this time. I find I tend to favour this kind of fast more than the other kinds of fasts. I find this kind of fast more enjoyable for me to do.

This is 24-hour a day fasting I am speaking about.

For example, going for three (3) days, or 72 hours, without eating or drinking any kind of food. Only consuming water for the entire water fast.

This is why it is called a water fast.

A centurion in the Bible called Cornelius did this type of fast. He did a water fast for over three (3) days.

In fact, it was on the fourth day of his fast that he had an angelic visitation.

Acts 10: 1 – 7 King James Version

10 There was a certain man in Caesarea called Cornelius, a centurion of the band called the Italian and,

² A devout man, and one that feared God with all his house, which gave much alms to the people, and prayed to God always.

³ He saw in a vision evidently about the ninth hour of the day an angel of God coming in to him, and saying unto him, Cornelius.

⁴ And when he looked on him, he was afraid, and said, What is it, Lord? And he said unto him, Thy prayers and thine alms are come up for a memorial before God.

⁵ And now send men to Joppa, and call for one Simon, whose surname is Peter:

⁶ He lodgeth with one Simon a tanner, whose house is by the sea side: he shall tell thee what thou oughtest to do.

⁷ And when the angel which spake unto Cornelius was departed, he called two of his household

servants, and a devout soldier of them that waited on him continually;…

The Lord Jesus Christ, Moses and Elijah had also done this kind of fast for 40 days and nights.

In the case of Moses, it was 40 days and nights without food and water on two successive occasions.

There are other kinds of fasts which are practiced today, but I have only shared a few of the more popular, biblical ones.

3. Esther Fast –

The Esther Fast is a biblical fast which Queen Esther and the Jews did. They fasted and prayed for three (3) days and nights (72 hours) without food and water to receive heavenly deliverance – To prevent them from being wiped out as a people.

Esther 4: 15, 16

¹⁵ Then Esther bade them return Mordecai this answer,

¹⁶ Go, gather together all the Jews that are present in Shushan, and **fast ye for me, and neither eat nor drink three days, night or day**: I also and my maidens will fast likewise; and so will I go in unto the king, which is not according to the law: and if I perish, I perish.

The Esther Fast had also been known to open up people's spiritual senses and caused them to see in the spirit realm.

However, it is advisable that this kind of fast should only be done if you had already done several water fasts.

The Apostle Paul and many other saints, past and present, also fasted often, and were blessed with an abundance of visions and revelations.

Fasting and Prayer subdues and denies the flesh and causes the person who is fasting to become more sensitive to the spirit realm.

What does Prayer and Fasting do?

a. It helps you to overcome temptation

Matthew 26:41

Watch and pray, that ye enter **not into temptation**: the spirit indeed is willing, but the flesh is weak.

Luke 22:40

And when he was at the place, he said unto them, Pray that ye enter **not into temptation**.

Mark 14: 38 King James Version

[38] Watch ye and pray, lest ye enter into temptation. The spirit truly is ready, but the flesh is weak.

Matthew 4: 1 to 3

4 Then was Jesus led up of the Spirit into the wilderness to be tempted of the devil.

[2] And when he had fasted forty days and forty nights, he was afterward an hungred.

³ And when the tempter came to him, he said, If thou be the Son of God, command that these stones be made bread.

Prayer and Fasting helps you to overcome temptation.

If Jesus, Himself, had to fast and pray, and fast and pray for 40 days and nights to overcome temptation and to prepare Him for ministry, what makes you think you can do otherwise, or anything less?

What makes you think that you don't have to fast?

We should be praying and fasting more often, since we know that one of the benefits of fasting and prayer is to overcome temptation.

Do you see the importance of prayer and fasting?

It helps you not to enter into temptation. It helps you to overcome temptation and the Devil. It is a security measure to prevent you from sinning.

This is why the Devil will fight to stop you from entering into a time and commitment of prayer and fasting, often.

He will give you all the 'seemingly legitimate reasons' why you should not fast, or get you to do a compromised version of a fast, which yields little to no fruit.

- **Prayer and Fasting helps you to become more sensitive to the presence of the Holy Spirit**

Yes, Fasting and Prayer does make you more sensitive to the presence of the Holy Spirit, but what does that mean in simple terms?

What does this church term mean 'more sensitive to the Spirit'?

Let me explain it this way, have you ever felt the presence of God?

Can you recall how that felt?

This is what that term, 'more sensitive to the Spirit' means in a nutshell.

It means you would be able to feel the presence of God more, and be in tune with the spirit realm.

This is both the good and evil spirit realms I am

speaking about.

You would be able to easily feel if an evil spirit is around, and you would be also able to easily feel if an angel is around.

Fasting and Prayer causes your spirit man to come to the fore, and your body and its soulish feelings to be subdued. You would have less desire for the flesh and the things of the world; and more desire for God and His Word.

Fasting and prayer increases your feelings of the presence of God, it increases your faith, it causes you to hear the voice of God easier and more often, and it increases the anointing of the Holy Spirit in you and upon you.

Fasting and Prayer also breaks every yoke.

Isaiah 58:6

Is not this the fast that I have chosen? to loose the bands of wickedness, to undo the heavy burdens, and to let the oppressed go free, and that ye **break every yoke**?

If fasting and prayer does these things and more, why

don't believers fast more often?

In fact, why don't you fast every day?

Don't you want to experience the presence of God more, and have your faith increased and every yoke broken?

How much do you love God?

How committed are you to Him?

How sold out to Him are you: 100%, 75%, 50%, 25%, 10%, less than that?

Truthfully and sincerely answer these questions before God.

I am asking you these questions because I want you to treat your salvation seriously and not frivolously.

I want you to become closer to Him than the very air that you breathe.

I want you to fulfill His purpose for the life He placed within you.

I want you to increase in favour with Him.

I want you to hear from Him on that accountable day

'Come you blessed of the Lord, enter into the Kingdom prepared for you." "Well done thou good and faithful servant."

Remember, Jesus Christ Himself had to fast and pray for forty (40) days and nights before He returned in the power of the Spirit. And never performed any miracles, not one, until He was tested in the wilderness by the Devil and fasted and prayed for 40 days and 40 nights.

Similarly, the apostles of the Lord Jesus Christ had to wait on the Lord in the upper room in fasting and prayer until the Holy Spirit came.

They were there for ten (10) days in prayer and fasting. Then they heard the sound of a mighty, rushing wind and their appeared cloven tongues of fire over each of them, and they were all baptized in the Holy Spirit and spoke in other tongues, and were empowered to be a witness for Him with signs, wonders and miracles accompanying their ministries.

Do you think you can have the same kind of success in ministry without doing what they did, without much fasting and prayer?

Does it matter how often and how long we fast and pray?

Of course, it does.

If it did not matter how long you fast, then Jesus would not have fasted for 40 day and 40 nights because those three (3) temptations listed there could have happened in the space of an hour or less.

In such a case, a one day fast of 24 hours without eating might have been more appropriate.

But why that was not the situation?

Why did He fasted for a specific number of days and nights – 40 days and 40 nights?

Why did Elijah fast for 40 days and nights?

Why did Moses fast 40 days and nights, twice, one after the other?

They all fasted for forty (40) days and nights because there is a power available and accessible to those who would venture to do so, which is more than what the average believer would receive or flow in when they receive Christ as their Saviour, and even after they are filled with the Holy Spirit with the evidence of speaking in other tongues.

Why should you fast _____ days and _____ nights to be empowered by the Holy Spirit for ministry?

(You can fill in the blank spaces above with the numbers)

- **Fasting breaks every yoke**

Isaiah 58:6

Is not this the fast that I have chosen? to loose the bands of wickedness, to undo the heavy burdens, and to let the oppressed go free, and that ye **break every yoke**?

Are you held in bondage by unseen chains, by relational, physical or spiritual yokes?

Fasting and Prayer will break every kind of bondage you are experiencing today.

Fasting and Prayer will break every yoke.

These are the meanings of the word 'yoke' taken form https://www.merriam-webster.com/dictionary/yoke

- wooden bar or frame by which two draft animals (such as oxen) are joined at the heads or necks for working together

- an arched device formerly laid on the neck of a defeated person.

- a frame fitted to a person's shoulders to carry a load in two equal portions

- **Fasting and Prayer helps you to receive guidance concerning major decisions**

Acts 13:1-3 King James Version

13 Now there were in the church that was at Antioch certain prophets and teachers; as Barnabas, and Simeon that was called Niger, and Lucius of Cyrene, and Manaen, which had been brought up with Herod the tetrarch, and Saul.

² As they ministered to the Lord, and fasted, the Holy Ghost said, Separate me Barnabas and Saul for the work whereunto I have called them.

³ And when they had fasted and prayed, and laid their hands on them, they sent them away.

Whenever the apostles had to make any serious decisions concerning a specific matter, they usually waited before God in fasting and prayer to receive guidance and an accurate word from the Lord.

- **Fasting and Prayer Empowers you**

⁸ But ye shall receive power, after that the Holy Ghost is come upon you: and ye shall be witnesses unto me both in Jerusalem, and in all Judaea, and in Samaria, and unto the uttermost part of the earth.

After fasting and praying for ten (10) days straight, the apostles were filled with the Holy Spirit and power – Power to be an effective witness for the Lord with signs, wonders and miracles following the preaching and teaching of the Word.

- **Fasting and Prayer wrought national deliverance for Israel in the days of Ester**

There is great power inherent in fasting and prayer - Enough power to change the degree of a notorious king… Great power to deliver an entire nation that was predetermined and decreed by the King and his right hand man for sure destruction – Obliteration…Power to return the intents and plans of the enemy, Hamon and his cohorts, on their own head.

You would have to read the whole book of Ester in the bible to get the entire picture of what transpired at that time.

Prayer and fasting has much more to do than just making you feel the presence of God more, or be more spiritually sensitive as believers say often.

The enemy knows that there is great power in-built in prayer and fasting, that is why he will try to deceive believers into thinking and believing that fasting is not that important, that it is just to make you feel the presence of God a little more, and then deceive you to make light of it.

Far from it my friend, a pure, blatant lie of the devil. A trick to rock believers into a sleep, while he roams freely, carrying out his intents, strategies and plans on the earth with little to no resistance from believers.

My friend, do you think you can dislodge the ancient rulers of darkness over continents, nations and countries, who have been ruling there for hundreds and thousands of years by just making some confessions and declarations?

If you think you will, you will soon find out how ineffective those declarations are without being backed up by serious prayers and fastings.

What you are really doing, unconsciously, when you abort your responsibility, when you fail to pray and fast, often, as watchmen and watchwomen over homes, communities, countries, nations and continents is, you have abandoned your post and put more pressure on a committed few to take up the slack, stand in the gap and void created by your absence, and man the stations you have deserted…. to pray and fast, day and night, for the concerns of the Lord Jesus Christ.

While you are sitting on your couch with popcorn in hand, watching a two (2) hour long movie which adds nothing to the Kingdom of God.

This is a sign of pure laziness, and a lack of love and care for the things of God.

This is sign that you as a watchman or watchwoman (every believer has this responsibility to be a watchman or watchwoman) have been lulled by the enemy into deep slumber and deception.

I implore of you switch off that television, put down that knife and spoon, turn over that plate and cup, and commit yourself to a time of fasting and prayer, now.

Millions of souls are being plunged into a Christ-less eternity, worldwide, every month, while you are living in wanton pleasure.

- **Fasting and Prayer empowers you to cast out certain kinds of devils**

Mark 9: 14 – 30 King James Version

> [14] And when he came to his disciples, he saw a

great multitude about them, and the scribes questioning with them.

¹⁵ And straightway all the people, when they beheld him, were greatly amazed, and running to him saluted him.

¹⁶ And he asked the scribes, What question ye with them?

16 And one of the multitude answered and said, Master, I have brought unto thee my son, which hath a dumb spirit;

¹⁸ And wheresoever he taketh him, he teareth him: and he foameth, and gnasheth with his teeth, and pineth away: and I spake to thy disciples that they should cast him out; and they could not.

¹⁹ He answereth him, and saith, O faithless generation, how long shall I be with you? how long shall I suffer you? bring him unto me.

²⁰ And they brought him unto him: and when he saw him, straightway the spirit tare him; and he

fell on the ground, and wallowed foaming.

²¹ And he asked his father, How long is it ago since this came unto him? And he said, Of a child.

²² And oft times it hath cast him into the fire, and into the waters, to destroy him: but if thou canst do any thing, have compassion on us, and help us.

²³ Jesus said unto him, If thou canst believe, all things are possible to him that believeth.

²⁴ And straightway the father of the child cried out, and said with tears, Lord, I believe; help thou mine unbelief.

²⁵ When Jesus saw that the people came running together, he rebuked the foul spirit, saying unto him, Thou dumb and deaf spirit, I charge thee, come out of him, and enter no more into him.

²⁶ And the spirit cried, and rent him sore, and came out of him: and he was as one dead; insomuch that many said, He is dead.

²⁷ But Jesus took him by the hand, and lifted him up; and he arose.

²⁸ And when he was come into the house, his disciples asked him privately, Why could not we cast him out?

²⁹ And he said unto them, **This kind can come forth by nothing, but by prayer and fasting.**

³⁰ And they departed thence, and passed through Galilee; and he would not that any man should know it.

There are certain kinds of demonic spirits which will not leave a person without prayer and fasting.

There are specific spirits which you would not be able to cast out without prayer and fasting.

Don't wait until you encounter them before you apply

Prayer and Fasting.

Be proactive and fast and pray often, now, so you would not have to try to do it when you are confronted with spiritual scenarios, which would warrant prayer and fasting.

I encourage you to fast and pray every day, and not wait until you are facing some kind of adversity before you do.

I would like to give another word of advice concerning prayer and fasting, here - Never allow your eating times to exceed your fasting times.

Don't eat more than you fast and pray.

You can serve God with Daily Prayer and Fasting

Luke 2:36-38
King James Version

36 And there was one Anna, a prophetess, the daughter of Phanuel, of the tribe of Aser: she was of a great age, and had lived with an husband seven years from her virginity;

37 And **she** was a widow of about fourscore and four

years, which departed not from the temple, but **served God with fastings and prayers night and day.**

[38] And she coming in that instant gave thanks likewise unto the Lord, and spake of him to all them that looked for redemption in Jerusalem.

Do you understand why Anna was a prophetess?

She was able to see and know things supernaturally because she fasted and prayed every day.

She Fasted every day. And she Prayed every day. She did this night and day, every day.

Pray and fast more than you eat and drink. This is not a commandment. This is godly advice.

Spend more hours each day without eating and drinking, than you spend with eating and drinking.

For example: you can refrain from eating and drinking anything for 12 hours or more each day.

In other words you fast for 12 hours or more each day.

Having said that, I can almost hear you say,

"What!"

I can't do that.

"I want scripture and verse for that."

"I have to be led by the Holy Spirit to do that."

"In fact, I have to be led by the Holy Spirit to do any kind of fast I undertake.""

If that be the case, tell me when was the last time or times the Holy Spirit led you into a fast or fasts?

If you have to wait until you are led by the Holy Spirit to fast and pray, you will hardly ever fast and pray, if you do.

And if you are honest with me, you will agree with me that is true.

The Lord has already stated and commanded in His Word that believers would fast after He had resurrected and returned to the Father.

And nowhere in the bible does it say that you have to be led of the Spirit before you fast. Absolutely nowhere.

What people have mistakenly misinterpreted for this wrong teaching is the scripture verse which states in

Matthew 4: 1, 2

¹ Then was Jesus led up of the Spirit into the wilderness to be tempted of the devil.

² And when he had fasted forty days and forty nights, he was afterward an hungred.

Believers have falsely interpreted this verse of scripture Matthew 4: 1 to mean that Jesus was led of the Spirit into the wilderness to fast and pray...

I want you to go back and reread those verses a few times and tell me what it really says.

It says, Jesus was led of the Spirit into the wilderness to be tempted of the devil

What it does not say is that Jesus was led of the Spirit into the wilderness to fast and pray.

It says that Jesus was led of the Spirit into the wilderness to be tempted of the devil; and in those days he fasted.

My friend, don't allow the devil to rob you out of a weapon the Lord has given to the church to destroy, pull down and uproot the kingdom of darkness from individuals, homes, communities and nations.

Prayer and Fasting is one of those powerful weapons that can greatly impact upon and destroy the kingdom of darkness.

This is why the devil would use all kinds of wrong teachings to deceive believers to think that fasting and prayer is not that important, and does nothing more than to cause one to feel or be more sensitive to the presence of God.

The devil knows your flesh would not want you to fast and prayer, often. And he would furnish you with all the reasons why you should not fast and prayer, often.

If you are honest with yourself you would agree with me that the real reason why you don't want to pray and fast, often is because:

- It feels uncomfortable. And you only want to do for God what feels comfortable and good.

- You are addicted to food and don't even realize it, until you are encouraged to fast and pray, often.

- You love food more than you love God.

- You just want to live a nominal Christian life.

- You get headaches when you fast. Do you know almost everyone who when they first began to practice fasting would have also experienced headaches, too?

   This usually happens because your body is getting rid of toxins in your body, and because you don't drink enough water when fasting to get rid of it, you may experience headaches.

Do not be deceived, I encourage you again:

Fast and Pray, often.

Chapter 9
Sanctify Yourself

What does sanctification have to do with seeing in the spirit?

Actually, a lot.

In the book of Leviticus in the Bible, God told Moses to tell the people that He wanted to meet with them, and that He was coming unto him (Moses) in a thick cloud, to speak to him audibly for all the people to hear Him speaking to him (Moses) and to see the thick cloud through which God would speak unto Moses, so that they would hear and believe the words that Moses speak unto them.

But He instructed Moses that before He could come and do so, the people had to sanctify themselves. He told Moses to tell the people what they had to do to sanctify themselves before He could come and speak with them directly.

Moses was supposed to have them sanctified by

telling them what the Lord required of them to do before He would consider them sanctified.

They had to sanctify themselves by doing certain things.

- They had to wash their clothes.

- They had to sleep separately from their wives for three (3) days before their meeting with God. They could not have sexual relations with their wife during those three (3) days.

- They could not come up the mountain when God come down in a thick cloud.

- They could not touch the bottom of the mountain when God came down.

- Not even the animals can touch the bottom of the mountain or go up the mountain when God came down.

This is what happened when God did came down

on the mount:

Exodus 19: 9 to 11, 16 to 19   KJV

⁹ And the LORD said unto Moses, Lo, I come unto thee in a thick cloud, **that the people may hear when I speak** with thee, and believe thee for ever. And Moses told the words of the people unto the LORD.

¹⁰ And the LORD said unto Moses, Go unto the people, and sanctify them to day and to morrow, and let them wash their clothes,

¹¹ And be ready against the third day:for the third day **the LORD will come down in the sight of all the people** upon mount Sinai.

¹⁶ And it came to pass on the third day in the morning, that there were **thunders and lightnings, and a thick cloud upon the mount, and the voice of the trumpet exceeding loud**; so that **all the people that was in the camp trembled.**

¹⁷ And Moses brought forth the people out of the camp to meet with God; and they stood at the nether part of the mount.

¹⁸ And mount Sinai was altogether on a smoke, because the LORD **descended upon it in fire: and the smoke thereof ascended as the smoke of a furnace, and the whole mount quaked greatly.**

¹⁹ And when the voice of the trumpet sounded long, and waxed louder and louder, Moses spake, and God answered him by a voice.

If God appeared visibly within a thick cloud, spoke audibly, and showed a measure of His glory for all the children of Israel to hear with their physical ears and to see with their physical eyes, to have a pillar of cloud go before them every day, and to have a pillar of fire protect them every night, and to eat angels' food seven (7) days every week under the Old Covenant, don't you know that He longs to show His glory to you, to all believers under the

New Covenant just like He did with the children of Israel under the Old Covenant?

Under the Old Covenant the children of Israel saw in the spirit realm every day for forty (40) years.

They received and ate angels' food from heaven for seven (7) days every week it fell in their camp.

They saw the pillar of fire ever night and the pillar of cloud every day, and they did not think it was something strange.

After a while it became natural for them to see and eat angels' food, see the pillar of cloud by day and the pillar of fire by night.

Exodus 13: 21, 22.

21 And the LORD went before them by day in a pillar of cloud to lead them along the way, and by night in a pillar of fire to give them light, that they might travel by day and by night. **22** The pillar of cloud by day and the pillar of fire by night did not depart from before the people.

Under the New Covenant, we too, should be experiencing seeing and hearing in the spirit realm, every day. It supposed to be as natural as breathing air is to us. But like the children of Israel, you too, have to sanctify yourself. You have to get rid of things which are hindering and blocking you from seeing and hearing in the spirit realm.

The word 'sanctify means to set apart to a sacred purpose, to free from sin, declare holy; consecrate.

There are two (2) types of Sanctification:

1. **The sanctification which you receive when you accept the Lord Jesus Christ** as your Lord and Saviour.

   This is sanctification of the spirit – Your spirit. **This sanctification comes from God.**

Jude 1:1

Jude, the servant of Jesus Christ, and brother of

James, to them that are **sanctified by God the Father**, and preserved in Jesus Christ, and called:

1 Corinthians 1:2   KJV

Unto the church of God which is at Corinth, to them that are **sanctified in Christ Jesus**, called to be saints, with all that in every place call upon the name of Jesus Christ our Lord, both theirs and ours:

1 Corinthians 6:11   KJV

And such were some of you: but ye are washed, but ye are **sanctified**, but ye are justified in the name of the Lord Jesus, and by the Spirit of our God.

Romans 15:16   KJV

That I should be the minister of Jesus Christ to the Gentiles, ministering the gospel of God that the offering up of the Gentiles might be acceptable, being **sanctified by the Holy Ghost.**

1 Corinthians 1:30   KJV

But of him are ye in Christ Jesus, who of God is

made unto us wisdom, and righteousness, and **sanctification**, and redemption:

2. **The second type of sanctification** is the one you have to apply daily to remain separated unto Him. **This is sanctification of the soul** (your soul consists of your mind, will and emotions) **and body.**

Sanctification of your soul is inner sanctification. Sanctification of your body is outer sanctification.

You need to apply both kinds of sanctification.

This is the second kind of sanctification or separation for the Lord. It is the one where **you have to sanctify yourself daily by separating yourself wholly to the Lord**,

The children of Israel, they had to sanctify themselves before God could have visited them.

Don't you know you too, would have to sanctify your soul and body if you expect a visit from God?

How do you sanctify your soul?

Sanctification of your soul is inner sanctification.

- ✓ **You sanctify your soul (mind, will and emotions)** when you read and listen to the Word of God often.

John 17:17

Sanctify them through **thy truth**: **thy word is truth**.

John 15:3

Now ye **are clean through the word** which I have spoken unto **you**.

- ✓ **You sanctify your soul (your mind, will and emotions)** when you renew your mind with the Word of God. When your thinking is governed by the Word of God.

Romans 12:2

And be not conformed to this world: but be ye

transformed by the **renewing of your mind**, that ye may prove what is that good, and acceptable, and perfect, will **of** God.

- ✓ **You sanctify your soul (your mind, will and emotions)** when you obey the Word of God.

2 Corinthians 10: 5, 6

⁵ Casting down imaginations, and every high thing that exalteth itself against the knowledge of God, and bringing into captivity every thought to the obedience of Christ;

⁶ And having in a readiness to revenge all disobedience, when your obedience is fulfilled.

You practically sanctify your mind, will and emotions:

- When you abstain from wrong company.

- When you stop watching and listening to

negative things about other ministers of God. This exposure pollutes your thinking and believing.

- When you stop listening to negative things said about people. This also pollutes your thinking and believing.

- Limit your time on the internet. When you Limit your surfing on the internet or search engines.

- When you limit your social media times. Latest data reveals that the typical working-age internet user now spends more than 2½ hours per day using social platforms, which is up by 2 percent (+3 minutes) compared with the daily average that the company reported at the start of 2022.

    https://datareportal.com/reports/digital-2023-deep-dive-time-spent-on-social-media

- Limit your hearing and reading of the news

Luke 21:26   KJV

Men's **hearts failing them** for fear, and for looking after those things which are coming on the earth: for the powers of heaven shall be shaken.

Data discloses that American adults spend more than 11 hours per day watching, reading, listening to, or simply interacting with media.

The average time spent consuming news is about 70 minutes per day.

https://thinkbynumbers.org/statistics/how-much-time-do-people-spend-consuming-news/

How do you sanctify your body?

You sanctify your body when you do not submit your body to fornication or the lusts of the flesh or put unwanted things in your body (alcohol, marijuana, and other products which are dangerous to and for your body).

1 Corinthians 6:13   KJV

Meats for the belly, and the belly for meats: but God shall destroy both it and them. **Now the body is not for fornication, but for the Lord;** and the Lord for the body

Corinthians 6:18   KJV

Flee fornication. Every sin that a man doeth is without the body; but **he that committeth fornication sinneth against his own body.**

1 Thessalonians 4: 1 to 7   KJV

4 Furthermore then we beseech you, brethren, and exhort you by the Lord Jesus, that as ye have received of us how ye ought to walk and to please God, so ye would abound more and more.

² For ye know what commandments we gave you by the Lord Jesus.

³ **For this is the will of God, even your sanctification that ye should abstain from fornication:**

⁴ That every one of you should know how to possess his vessel in sanctification and honour;

⁵ Not in the lust of concupiscence, even as the Gentiles which know not God:

⁶ That no man go beyond and defraud his brother in any matter: because that the Lord is the avenger of all such, as we also have forewarned you and testified.

⁷ For God hath not called us unto uncleanness, but unto holiness.

You sanctify your body by staying away from all forms of sexual sins.

When Samson's mother got word from an angel that she would have a son who would be a Nazarite and a deliverer of Israel, he warned her not to drink wine or strong drink.

She was supposed to sanctify herself and the child even from the womb by not drinking wine and strong drink, and not eating anything unclean.

Judges 13: 3 to 5

³ And the angel of the LORD appeared unto the woman, and said unto her, Behold now, thou art barren, and bearest not: but thou shalt conceive, and bear a son.

⁴ Now therefore beware, I pray thee, and **drink not wine nor strong drink,** and **eat not any unclean thing:**

⁵ For, lo, thou shalt conceive, and bear a son; and no razor shall come on his head: for the child shall be a Nazarite unto God from the womb: and he shall begin to deliver Israel out of the hand of the Philistines.

You are also commanded by God to sanctify yourself.

You also sanctify your body:

- **When you sanctify your eyes.** When you stop using your eyes to look at what you should not be looking at. Stop looking at movies and shows you should not be looking at. Stop looking at pornography.

- **When you sanctify your ears.** When you stop using your ears to listen to and hear wrong things.

   Stop allowing your ears to hear news of bloodshed. Stop listening to and reading news which talks about killings and murders and bloodshed.

Isaiah 33: 14, 15   KJV

[14] Who among us can dwell with that devouring fire? Who among us can dwell with those everlasting burnings?

[15] He who walks righteously and speaks uprightly …he **who stops his ears from hearing of bloodshed** and shuts his eyes to avoid looking upon evil.

Just to recap:

    a. You need to sanctify yourself to see in the spirit realm. You need to remove all things which could be hindering and blocking you from seeing in the spirit.

    b. There are 2 types of sanctification:

1. Sanctification of your spirit. This is the sanctification you receive when you accept Jesus Christ as the Lord and Saviour of your life. The Heavenly Father does this sanctification for you through His Holy Spirit when you are born again.

2. The sanctification of your soul and body, which you are responsible for. Your soul consists of your mind, will and emotions.

    ○ This sanctification of the soul involves inner sanctification - The sanctifying of your mind, will and emotions. This includes: Reading and listening to the Word of God, Renewing your mind with the Word of God, and Obeying the

Word of God.

- The sanctification of the body involves outer sanctification – Abstaining from sexual sins and the lusts of the flesh.

- You can also sanctify your body by protecting what you allow your eyes to see and what you allow your ears to hear.

- Stop listening to news about killings, murders and violence. The bible instructs us to stop reading about bloodshed, and stop allowing our ears to hear about violence and bloodshed.

And every man that hath this hope in him purifieth himself, even as he is **pure**. 1 John 3:3

My friend, sanctify yourself. Keep yourself pure.

Chapter 10
Speaking in Tongues

What is speaking in tongues?

Speaking in tongues is speaking in another language which you have not learned through the power of the Holy Spirit, as the Spirit gives you utterance.

It is not a learnt language.

When the Lord baptized His disciples with the Holy Spirit and fire on the day of Pentecost in the upper room, they all spoke with other tongues, languages which they had not learned, as the Spirit gave them utterance.

What does speaking in other tongues have to do with seeing in the spirit?

Many believers had begun seeing in the spirit realm after they spoke in tongues for four (4) continuous hours and more - Their spiritual eyes were opened.

You would have to plan for this one, though, as it involves several continuous hours of praying in tongues, at once.

Organize a specific time and place in the day when you can do this without distractions.

I am not talking about doing this once as a trial.

I am speaking about doing this for at least 30 consecutive days or more - Actually, making it a lifestyle.

Please bear in mind, it will take some determination for you to follow through with this practice, but stick with it.

There are two (2) kinds of tongues spoken of in Scripture:

1. Tongues which we pray in our private prayer time. This is the personal prayer language which is given to benefit you, the believer, to enable you to communicate with God on a higher level.

2. The gift of tongues with interpretation which is used to convey a prophetic word to the church. These utterances were given to benefit the body of Christ.

So one kind of tongues is used for your private, personal prayer time with the Lord.

And the other kind of tongues is used for Ministry, to benefit other believers in the body of Christ.

What is the purpose of speaking in tongues?

1. Speaking in other tongues is evidence that one has been filled with or baptized in the Holy Spirit.

Acts 2: 1 to 4

And when the day of Pentecost was fully come, they were all with one accord in one place.

[2] And suddenly there came a sound from heaven as of a rushing mighty wind, and it filled all the house

where they were sitting.

³ And there appeared unto them cloven tongues like as of fire, and it sat upon each of them.

⁴ And they were all filled with the Holy Ghost, and began to speak with other tongues, as the Spirit gave them utterance.

Acts 10: 44 to 46

⁴⁴ While Peter yet spake these words, the Holy Ghost fell on all them which heard the word.

⁴⁵ And they of the circumcision which believed were astonished, as many as came with Peter, because that on the Gentiles also was poured out the gift of the Holy Ghost.

⁴⁶ For they heard them speak with tongues, and magnify God.

Acts 19: 1 to 7

And it came to pass, that, while Apollos was at

Corinth, Paul having passed through the upper coasts came to Ephesus: and finding certain disciples,

² He said unto them, Have ye received the Holy Ghost since ye believed? And they said unto him, We have not so much as heard whether there be any Holy Ghost.

³ And he said unto them, Unto what then were ye baptized? And they said, Unto John's baptism.

⁴ Then said Paul, John verily baptized with the baptism of repentance, saying unto the people, that they should believe on him which should come after him, that is, on Christ Jesus.

⁵ When they heard this, they were baptized in the name of the Lord Jesus.

⁶ And when Paul had laid his hands upon them, the Holy Ghost came on them; and they spake with tongues, and prophesied.

⁷ And all the men were about twelve.

> 2. Speaking in tongues is speaking directly to God.

For **he that speaketh in an unknown tongue speaketh not unto men, but unto God:** for no man understandeth him; howbeit in the spirit he speaketh mysteries.

1 Corinthians 14:2 King James Version

For **one who speaks in an [unknown] tongue speaks not to men but to God**, for no one understands or catches his meaning, because in the [Holy] Spirit he utters secret truths *and* hidden things [not obvious to the understanding].

1 Corinthians 14:2 Amplified Bible Translation, Classic Version.

> 3. Speaking in other tongues recharges the believer's spirit.

1 Corinthians 14: 4 King James Version

He that speaketh in an unknown tongue edifieth himself...

Jude 1: 20 Amplified Bible Translation, Classic

But you, beloved, build yourselves up [founded] on your most holy faith [make progress, rise like an edifice higher and higher], praying in the Holy Spirit;

When you speak in unknown tongues you edify or build up your spirit man.

This is another purpose used by God to build you up on the inside, in your spirit.

If you speak in unknown tongues, you will notice after speaking in tongues that you feel lifted up, stronger, and encouraged on the inside of you.

It is a spiritual exercise for your spirit to become stronger.

This is another reason why you should speak in

tongues often, and for long periods, particularly if you want to have more spiritual experiences.

There are many more beneficial reasons why you should speak in other tongues often, and for long periods of time but I cannot go into them now.

However, in the near future I trust I would be able to share them all with you.

As I close this chapter let me remind you that many believers has spoken in tongues for over four (4) hours at a time and had their spiritual eyes opened to see in the spirit realm.

What about you?

Don't you think it's time for you to explore all these benefits of the spirit available to you?

How about dedicating four (4) solid hours of praying in tongues each day for thirty (30) days straight?

That would be a good spiritual experiment to conduct.

Questions and Answers:

Question 1: Should everyone speak in tongues?

Answer: Yes, every believer should speak with other tongues.

Question 2: Is speaking in tongues a spiritual gift which only some receive, or is it a gift available for all?

Answer: Speaking in tongues is a spiritual gift given by God for everyone.

Yes, speaking in tongues is for everyone.

Question 3: How do you receive this spiritual gift?

Answer: Simple. You ask God in prayer to fill you with His Holy Spirit, thank Him by faith for doing so, and then open your mouth and expect to praise the Lord in another language.

Please don't wait passively and expect the Holy Spirit to take control of your tongue and vocal chords and make you speak in other tongues, while you witness all this as a passive bystander.

You have an active part to play.

You have to use your will and speak first, expecting that as you open your mouth and speak by faith - The Holy Spirit will give you a new prayer language, which is known as 'speaking in tongues'.

My friend, there is a lot more which can be said about speaking in tongues, but I have only written a concise version of it.

Chapter 11
Walk in the Spirit

If you walk consistently in the Spirit you would almost without effort, also see in the spirit realm.

If you consistently walk in the Spirit every day, you would without fail, see in the spirit realm. Because you are practicing virtues which are not of this world, but virtues which are directly from and belong to heaven…virtues which come from the heart of God and which are a part of His nature.

I know you want to see and hear in the spirit all the time, but are you willing to walk in the spirit all the time?

Walking in the Spirit Daily means to walk, live, exhibit, and exude the fruit of the Spirit all the time.

Do you know what the fruit of the Spirit is?

Do you know what the bible says is the fruit of the

Spirit but do not practice it?

Do you know once you practice the fruit of the Spirit, daily (virtues which are listed in Galatians 5: 22 to 25) the spirit realm would automatically open up to you.

You would not even have to pray for God to activate your spiritual senses.

How do you walk in the Spirit?

How do you walk in the virtues which belong to God?

You practice the fruit of the Spirit, daily.

According to Almighty God, this is what it means to be walking in the Spirit. This is what God terms 'Living in the Spirit.

It is not what we think.

It is not demonstrating the gifts of the Spirit.

The gifts of the Spirit and the Fruit of the Spirit are two separate things. They are not the same.

Walking in the Spirit is not demonstrating the prophetic or power gifts of the Spirit, many have been deceived into thinking that it is, this is why they are passionately pursuing the gifts of the Spirit (and paying false prophets money to have these gifts transferred to them), but have very little fruit of the Spirit to carry those gifts.

Operating in supernatural gifts like healing the sick, prophecy, preaching, etc. is not evidence that you are walking in the Spirit - That is not proof that you are living in the Spirit.

Walking in the Spirit, according to God, means practicing and demonstrating the fruit of the Spirit which is found in Galatians 5: 22, 23, this is what you will be rewarded for in heaven at the judgment seat of Christ.

Galatians 5:22, 23

[22] But the fruit of the Spirit is love, joy, peace, longsuffering, gentleness, goodness, faithfulness,

²³ Meekness, temperance: against such there is no law.

Galatians 5:16

This I say then, **Walk in the Spirit**, and ye shall not fulfil **the lust of the flesh.**

Galatians 5:25

If we live in **the Spirit**, let us also **walk** in **the Spirit**.

Galatians 5: 22 – 24 Amplified Bible Translation Classic

²² But the fruit of the [Holy] Spirit [the work which His presence within accomplishes] is love, joy (gladness), peace, patience (an even temper, forbearance), kindness, goodness (benevolence), faithfulness,

²³ Gentleness (meekness, humility), self-control (self-restraint, continence). Against such things there is no law [that can bring a charge].

[24] And those who belong to Christ Jesus (the Messiah) 'have crucified the flesh (the godless human nature) with its passions and appetites *and* desires.

(I will do another book which goes into much details about the fruit of the Spirit. But I will just give a synopsis of it for now)

There are 9 character traits of the Fruit of the Spirit.

Please note it is singular, Fruit, not Fruits of the Spirit in Galatians 5: 22. One Fruit, but 9 manifestations or character traits of that Fruit, the Fruit of the Spirit.

1. Love

Galatians 5: 22

But the fruit of the Spirit is Love……

What is Love?

In the Greek language, there are 4 different words used to define 4 types of Love.

The Love which the Bible is referring to in Galatians 5 is called in the Greek language 'Agape'. It is defined as the 'God type of Love'.

This God-Love or God kind of Love is

- Longsuffering
- Patient and Kind
- It is not envious of others or jealous of others.
- It is not boastful, prideful or vain.
- It is not unmannerly,
- It does not insist on its own way
- t is not selfish, or seeks to promote itself
- It is not touchy, fretful or resentful.

John 13:34

A new commandment I give unto you, that ye love one another; as I have loved you, that ye also love one another.

1 Corinthians chapter 13 is a whole chapter which is

dedicated to telling you what 'Agape' love, the God-kind of love looks like.

I cannot go into details about the God kind of Love here because it is a big subject which would require an entire book by itself to do it justice.

1 Corinthians 13
Amplified Bible Translation, Classic Edition

13 If I [can] speak in the tongues of men and [even] of angels, but have not love (that reasoning, intentional, spiritual devotion such [a]as is inspired by God's love for and in us), I am only a noisy gong or a clanging cymbal.

2 And if I have prophetic powers ([b]the gift of interpreting the divine will and purpose), and understand all the secret truths *and* mysteries and possess all knowledge, and if I have [sufficient] faith so that I can remove mountains, but have not love (God's love in me) I am nothing (a useless nobody).

³ Even if I dole out all that I have [to the poor in providing] food, and if I surrender my body to be burned *or* [c]*in order that I may glory*, but have not love (God's love in me), I gain nothing.

⁴ Love endures long *and* is patient and kind; love never is envious *nor* boils over with jealousy, is not boastful *or* vainglorious, does not display itself haughtily.

⁵ It is not conceited (arrogant and inflated with pride); it is not rude (unmannerly) *and* does not act unbecomingly. Love (God's love in us) does not insist on its own rights *or* its own way, *for* it is not self-seeking; it is not touchy *or* fretful *or* resentful; it takes no account of the evil done to it [it pays no attention to a suffered wrong].

⁶ It does not rejoice at injustice *and* unrighteousness but rejoices when right *and* truth prevail.

⁷ Love bears up under anything *and* everything that comes, is ever ready to believe the best of every person, its hopes are fadeless under all

circumstances, and it endures everything [without weakening].

⁸ Love never fails [never fades out or becomes obsolete or comes to an end]. As for prophecy (the gift of interpreting the divine will and purpose), it will be fulfilled *and* pass away; as for tongues, they will be destroyed *and* cease; as for knowledge, it will pass away [it will lose its value and be superseded by truth].

⁹ For our knowledge is fragmentary (incomplete and imperfect), and our prophecy (our teaching) is fragmentary (incomplete and imperfect).

¹⁰ But when the complete *and* perfect (total) comes, the incomplete *and* imperfect will vanish away (become antiquated, void, and superseded).

¹¹ When I was a child, I talked like a child, I thought like a child, I reasoned like a child; now that I have become a man, I am done with childish ways *and* have put them aside.

¹² For now we are looking in a mirror that gives only a dim (blurred) reflection [of reality as in a riddle or enigma], but then [when perfection comes] we shall see in reality *and* face to face! Now I know in part (imperfectly), but then I shall know and understand fully *and* clearly, even in the same manner as I have been fully *and* clearly known *and* understood [by God].

¹³ And so faith, hope, love abide [faith—conviction and belief respecting man's relation to God and divine things; hope—joyful and confident expectation of eternal salvation; love—true affection for God and man, growing out of God's love for and in us], these three; but the greatest of these is love.

2. Joy

Joy is beyond happiness. True joy is not dependent on beautiful things, money or blissful events.

True joy comes from your relationship with the Lord Jesus Christ.

Joy is a character trait of the fruit of the Holy Spirit.

Nehemiah 8: 10

…for **the joy of the Lord** is your strength.

There are times when joy is a sacrifice.

Let me explain what I mean.

Some years ago, in the month of December, myself and my family were going through some trying times….we had almost no food to eat and no money to buy groceries or money to cover our monthly expenses, plus we were told by the landlords that we would have to leave the apartment we were staying in if we could not pay the rent; but myself and my wife made a conscious decision to march around our living room area, despite all we were facing and praise the Lord - To offer Him the sacrifice of praise, of joy, of thanksgiving for all He had done for us….(we were literally enjoying those moments of joy).

When we praised the Lord, sacrificially, the Lord Jesus then put His joy into our hearts, laughter in our mouths, and encouragement and faith in our souls, and believe it or not, things actually turned around that very day through a series of supernatural miracles.

All those details would be placed in another book suitable for these stories of faith, though.

Psalm 27:6

And now shall mine head be lifted up above mine enemies round about me: therefore will I offer in his tabernacle **sacrifices of joy**; I will sing, yea, I will sing praises unto the LORD.

John 15:11

These things have I spoken unto you, that my **joy** might remain in you, and that your **joy** might be full.

John 16:24

Hitherto have ye asked nothing in my name: ask, and ye shall receive, that your **joy** may be full.

The Lord Jesus Christ wants us to have and live with fullness of joy. And a part of having your joy full comes from asking the Heavenly Father for what we need or require in the name of the Lord Jesus Christ and we will receive them.

Psalm 5:11

But let all those that put their trust in thee rejoice: **let them ever shout for joy**, because thou defendest them: let them also that love thy name be **joy**ful in thee.

The joy of the Lord also comes by rejoicing in the Lord by faith. You don't have to wait until you feel joyful to praise the Lord. If you praise Him and rejoice in Him by faith you would receive His joy.

Psalm 16:11

Thou wilt shew me the path of life: in thy presence is fulness of **joy**; at thy right hand there are pleasures for evermore.

When we spend quality time in the presence of God, lingering in His presence in prayer, fellowship and love for Him, He releases to us the fullness of His joy.

Psalm 32:11

Be glad in the LORD, and rejoice, ye righteous: and shout for **joy**, all ye that are upright in heart.

Psalm 63:5

My soul shall be satisfied as with marrow and fatness; and my mouth shall praise thee with **joy**ful lips:

Psalm 66:1

Make a **joy**ful noise unto God, all ye lands:

Psalm 81:1

Sing aloud unto God our strength: make a **joy**ful noise unto the God of Jacob.

Psalm 95:1

O come, let us sing unto the LORD: let us make a **joy**ful noise to the rock of our salvation.

Psalm 95:2

Let us come before his presence with thanksgiving, and make a **joy**ful noise unto him with psalms.

Psalm 98:4

Make a **joy**ful noise unto the LORD, all the earth: make a loud noise, and rejoice, and sing praise.

Psalm 100:1

Make a **joy**ful noise unto the LORD, all ye lands.

Psalm 132:9

Let thy priests be clothed with righteousness; and **let thy saints shout for joy**.

Psalm 132:16

I will also clothe her priests with salvation: **and her saints shall shout aloud for joy.**

Psalm 149:5

Let the saints be joyful in glory: **let them sing aloud upon their beds.**

3. Peace

We are living in a world of toil, where to many, peace have been an elusive commodity within and without.

People, believers, are struggling to experience peace on the inside of them, and there is not much peace on the outside of them, also.

Do you experience peace even though there are lots of turmoil around you?

True peace can only be found in an intimate, up-to-date, ongoing relationship with the Lord Jesus Christ.

Peace, True Peace can be received by:

  a. Forming an intimate relationship with the Lord Jesus Christ.

John 14:27

Peace I leave with **you, my peace I give unto you**: not as the world **give**th, **give I unto you**. Let not **you**r heart be troubled, neither let it be afraid.

John 16:33

These things I have spoken unto you, that in me ye might have peace. In the world ye shall have tribulation: but be of good cheer; I have overcome the world.

    b. By casting all your cares, all the things which you are worried about upon Him, for He cares for you.

Philippians 4:6, 7

⁶ Be careful for nothing; but in every thing by prayer and supplication with thanksgiving let your requests be made known unto God.

⁷ And the peace of God, which passeth all understanding, shall keep your hearts and minds through Christ Jesus.

    c. Peace is an attribute of the Kingdom of God. The peace of God is the atmosphere of the Kingdom of God. The word of God states that the Kingdom of God is righteousness, Peace and Joy in the Holy Ghost.

Romans 14:17

For the kingdom of God is not meat and drink; but righteousness, and peace, and joy in the Holy Ghost.

d. Peace is a manifestation of the fruit of the Holy Spirit. Your life supposed to carry the Peace of God. People supposed to be able to sense the Peace of God exuding from you wherever you go or are. The Peace of God supposed to fill your home.

Galatians 5:22-23

But the fruit of the Spirit is love, joy, **peace**, patience, kindness, goodness, faithfulness, gentleness, self-control; against such things there is no law.

Colossians 3:15

And let the peace of God rule in your hearts, to the which also ye are called in one body; and be ye thankful.

Matthew 5:9

⁹ **Blessed are the peacemakers**: for they shall be called the children of God.

2 Corinthians 13:11

Finally, brethren, farewell. Be perfect, be of good comfort, be of one mind, **live in peace**; and the God of love and peace shall be with you.

4. Longsuffering

Longsuffering is suffering patiently for a long time without complaining, blaming God or others.

Do you demonstrate this manifestation of the fruit of the Spirit in your life?

It is suffering for things which are not your fault. It is suffering for doing well, for doing good for His sake.

For instance, being wrongfully accused of things you did not do or say, without trying to justify yourself, defend yourself and your reputation. But giving thanks in spite of what you are facing.

1 Peter 3: 17, 18

¹⁷ For it is better, if the will of God be so, that ye suffer for well doing, than for evil doing.

¹⁸ For Christ also hath once suffered for sins, the just for the unjust, that he might bring us to God, being put to death in the flesh, but quickened by the Spirit:

Ephesians **4: 1, 2**

4 I therefore, the prisoner of the Lord, beseech you that ye walk worthy of the vocation wherewith ye are \called,

² With all lowliness and meekness, **with**

longsuffering, forbearing one another in love;

³ Endeavouring to keep the unity of the Spirit in the bond of peace.

Colossians 3:12

Put on therefore, as the elect of God, holy and beloved, bowels of mercies, kindness, humbleness of mind, meekness, **longsuffering**;

5. Gentleness

Although I believe that you know what it means to be 'gentle' I will still share a little about 'gentleness'.

The apostle Paul in his inspired writing in 1 Thessalonians 2:7 gives us a vivid picture of what it means to be 'gentle'. He compares the gentleness they showed to the believers at Thessalonica as the kind of gentleness a mother breast-feeding her child, shows to her child.

Can you picture how gentle a nursing mother is with

her child?

This is the kind of gentleness God wants us to show to others.

1 Thessalonians 2:7

But we were **gentle** among you, even as a nurse cherisheth her children:

2 Timothy 2:24

And the servant of the Lord must not strive; but be **gentle** unto all men, apt to teach, patient,

Titus 3:2

To speak evil of no man, to be no brawlers, but **gentle**, shewing all meekness unto all men.

James 3:17

But the wisdom that is from above is first pure, then peaceable, **gentle**, and easy to be intreated, full of mercy and good fruits, without partiality, and without hypocrisy.

6. Goodness

Here are a few things which the Bible has to say about 'Goodness'. I cannot expound in details about them all.

However, I have shared a few:

- The word of God states it is the goodness of God which leads men to repentance.

Are you good to those around you?

Are you good to your wife / husband, children, siblings, mother, father, father-in-law, mother-in-law, co-workers, neighbours, friends, people who you don't know?

If you are good to those around you, especially to those who are not saved, they will want what you have, they will ask you questions about what makes you different.

- The word of God commands us to ….**Do good to those who hate you….**

Matthew 5:44 KJV

- But I say unto you, Love your enemies, bless them that curse you, **do good to them that hate you**, and pray for them which despitefully use you, and persecute you;

That verse above is not a typographical error, but a command from the Lord Jesus Christ, the head of the church.

Do you do well to those who hate you?

Remember, this scripture is stating actions here.

It means that if you know someone hates you, you are to do them good. You are to look for ways to do them good.

Meaning: it is not enough for you to say concerning those who hate you and don't like you, "I don't wish them bad. I don't have anything against them. I forgive them"

He, God, expects you to do something more, to **do**

something good for them. It could be sending them a gift, opening a door for them if you work at the same place they are working; it could be buying them a nice lunch and having it delivered to them….

It's your turn now to **find creative ways to do good to those who hate you.**

If you don't know what good thing to do for those who hate you, ask the Lord Jesus Christ to tell you what to do for them.

- Here is a biblical example of what being good looks like.

There are times when being good may seem unjust to those around you, especially in the working world, especially among unionized workers.

Matthew 20:15   KJV

Is it not lawful for me **to do** what I will with mine own? Is thine eye evil, because I am **good**?

In the book of Matthew, chapter 20, Jesus tells the

parable of a householder who had some work to be done in his vineyard, and went out and hired workers to come and work in his vineyard at different hours of the day.

He hired workers to work in his vineyard at the third hour.

He hired workers to work in his vineyard at the sixth hour.

He hired workers to work in his vineyard at the ninth hour.

He hired workers to work in his vineyard at the eleventh hour.

At the end of the working day he called all the workers to pay them their wage.

However, he paid every worker a penny, despite what time of the day they reported for work in the householder's field.

In our working day, that would seem quite unfair to you, right now as you are reading this, you are already thinking that is unfair.

But the Lord Jesus Christ did not think so. He thought the householder was being good, a good man to those workers.

That is why He said in His parable in our everyday language:

"Am I not allowed to do what I want with my money? And because this is my money, I can choose to give everybody the same wage regardless of what hour of the day they reported for work.

Jesus called what this man did 'Good'. Jesus inferred that this man was a good man.

Do you know what they would have called that householder in our day?

They would have called him unfair and a terrible boss to work for.

This is what the workers in the parable Jesus gave complained about, they reasoned and said, "How could the workers who came in the last hour of the day be paid the same wages as us who started to work at the beginning of the working day and borne the heat of the daylight sun.

Something wrong here."

(my paraphrased version)

I can only imagine that the workers union would have taken him to the industrial court for unfairness and demand that he give those workers fair wages for the work they performed.

It was like that when I worked with a reputable company several years ago as a temporary worker.

I was asked to do a so-called senior staff work for the company who lost a senior worker who had done the work before.

But I did not know how to do the job, and the supervisor of the department told me to ask the permanent co-workers who were in the department to show me what to do.

But when I went to them to ask them for that help they bluntly refused to show me.

I am telling you about persons who supposed to be believers in the Lord Jesus Christ.

They told me that is not their job. The company did not hire them to teach workers how to do the job.

But you know, I can hear some of you who are reading the previous paragraphs in this chapter say right now,

"They are right."

Yes, right.

But right in whose eyes?

The eyes of the working world?

They may be right in the eyes of the unions representing workers, but 100 percent wrong in God's eyes. The eyes of Him who see everything. And He who searches the earth to find a person/s whose heart is perfect towards Him, through whom He can show Himself strong.

I can tell you with complete accuracy that, that person would not be you, if you have that kind of mindset.

How do I know that?

Read what He said in Matthew 5:41

[41] And whosoever shall compel thee to go a mile, go with him twain.

In our modern day words, if you were ask to do something on the job, don't' only do what you were asked to do, go the extra mile.

Always go the extra mile on your job; not doing it for recognition or promotion, but doing it sincerely as unto the Lord. And the Lord who sees in secret will reward you openly.

This is an example of what the manifestation of fruit of the Spirit, 'goodness', looks like.

Proverbs 14:22

[22] Do they not err who devise evil *and* wander from the way of life? **But loving-kindness *and* mercy, loyalty *and* faithfulness, shall be to those who devise good.**

God has promised that He will give loving-kindness and mercy, to those who are good.

God has promised that He will be loyal and faithful to those who are good.

Galatians 6:9

And let us **not be weary in well doing**: for **in** due season we shall reap, if we faint **not**.

I know there are times when you may grow tired of doing good for others, especially if those people are ungrateful, or are people who try to use you to get as much as they can from you, and turned out to be scammers; but He has promised if you don't faint in doing good for others, you will reap. He will reward you accordingly.

Ephesians 5:9

(For the fruit of the Spirit is in all goodness and righteousness **and truth** ;)

Titus 3:8

This is a faithful saying, and these things I will that thou affirm constantly, that they which have believed in God might **be careful to maintain good works**. These things are good and profitable unto men.

Hebrews 13:16

But to **do good** and to communicate forget not: **for with such sacrifices God is well pleased.**

God is well pleased with those who are sacrificially doing good for others.

This is the praise He gave to His beloved Son when He was baptized by John the Baptist, "...This is my beloved Son in whom I am well pleased."

This is the same praise God the Father gives to those who are sacrificially and genuinely doing good for people, without fanfare, the desire to be praised, without doing it for others to see and give them praise, without expecting anything in return -

Persons who are just doing good for others because they love God and they love people.

3 John 1:11

Beloved, follow not that which is evil, but that which is good. **He that doeth good is of God**: but he that doeth evil hath not seen God.

The word of God states that he who does good, good things for others, is of God.

7. Faithfulness

Another manifestation of the fruit of the Spirit in Galatians 5:23 is Faithfulness. It is translated and written as Faith in the King James Version of the Bible. But it really comes from the Greek work 'Pistis' which means faithfulness.

The Bible states that God is faithful that promised, which means He is dependable, trustworthy and keeps His word, and expects us as His children to also operate the same way.

Are you a faithful person?

Are you reliable and dependable?

Do you keep your word?

Do you know part of faithfulness is keeping your word?

Faithfulness is a manifestation of the character of the Spirit of God, which means God is faithful, He is dependable, reliable, keeps His Word, and can be trusted; and as His children He expects us to exemplify the same qualities of faithfulness.

Lamentations 3:22, 23

[22] It is of the LORD's mercies that we are not consumed, because his compassions fail not.

[23] They are new every morning: great is thy **faithfulness.**

.Hosea 2:20

I will even betroth thee unto me in **faithfulness**: and

thou shalt know the LORD.

Psalm 36:5

Thy mercy, O LORD, is in the heavens; and thy **faithfulness** reacheth unto the clouds.

Psalm 89:1

I will sing of the mercies of the LORD for ever: with my mouth will I make known thy **faithfulness** to all generations.

Psalm 89:8

O LORD God of hosts, who is a strong LORD like unto thee? or to thy **faithfulness** round about thee?

Psalm 89:24

But my **faithfulness** and my mercy shall be with him: and in my name shall his horn be exalted.

Psalm 89:33

Nevertheless my lovingkindness will I not utterly take from him, nor suffer my **faithfulness** to fail.

Psalm 92:2

To shew forth thy lovingkindness in the morning, and thy **faithfulness** every night,

Psalm 119:90

Thy **faithfulness** is unto all generations: thou hast established the earth, and it abideth.

Isaiah 25:1

O Lord, thou art my God; I will exalt thee, I will praise thy name; for thou hast done wonderful things; thy counsels of old are **faithfulness** and truth.

8. Meekness

The word "meekness" in Galatians 5:23 comes from the Greek word *prautes*, which depicts *the attitude or demeanor of a person who is forbearing, patient, and slow to respond in anger*.

It pictures a strong-willed person who has learned to submit his will to a higher authority. He isn't *weak*; he is *controlled*. He may in fact possess a strong will and a powerful character, but this person has learned the secret of how to *bring his will under control.*

https://www.bible.com/reading-plans/24593-the-fruit-of-the-spirit-by-rick-renner/day/6

Meekness is not weakness. It is strength under control.

A vivid picture of meekness / self-control is the Lord Jesus Christ who humbly submitted Himself to be spitted on, slapped, ridiculed, taunted, have His beard plucked out, cursed, and cruelly beaten beyond recognition and nailed to a cross, …., who did not use or call upon the power which was available to Him to destroy all his detractors, persecutors and tormenters in a second is a perfect example of meekness, temperance and self-control.

His life is the measure we should seek to attain.

His works which He did when He walked the earth is what we should be duplicating.

The way He lived when He was on earth in bodily form is the life we ought to imitate.

Can you humbly suffer injustice without trying to justify or defend yourself?

Can you be ill-treated by others without retaliating?

If you were ill-treated by others would you retaliate?

If you were lied upon, verbally abused and your name be spoken of with disdain, would you seek to justify yourself and pray for retribution, or for God to justify you against those who had done you these wrongs?

In the book of Matthew 26:53 The Lord Jesus Christ said to His disciples after He was arrested, particularly to Peter who drew his sword and cut off an ear from one of the servants of the Pharisees to protect Jesus from being arrested.

Matthew 26:52-54 King James Version

⁵² Then said Jesus unto him, Put up again thy sword into his place: for all they that take the sword shall perish with the sword.

⁵³ Thinkest thou that I cannot now pray to my Father, and he shall presently give me more than twelve legions of angels?

⁵⁴ But how then shall the scriptures be fulfilled, that thus it must be?

Isaiah 53:7

He was oppressed, and he was afflicted, yet he opened not his mouth: he is brought as a lamb to the slaughter, and as a sheep before her shearers is dumb, so he openeth not his mouth.

Matthew 11:29

Take my yoke upon you, and learn of me; for I am meek and lowly in heart: and ye shall find rest unto your souls.

1 Peter 2:23

Who, when he was reviled, reviled not again; when he suffered, he threatened not; but committed himself to him that judgeth righteously:

1 Peter 3:13-22 King James Version

[13] And who is he that will harm you, if ye be followers of that which is good?

[14] **But and if ye suffer for righteousness' sake, happy are ye**: and be not afraid of their terror, neither be troubled;

[15] But sanctify the Lord God in your hearts: and be ready always to give an answer to every man that asketh you a reason of the hope that is in you with meekness and fear:

[16] Having a good conscience; that, whereas they speak evil of you, as of evildoers, they may be ashamed that falsely accuse your good conversation in Christ.

17 For it is better, if the will of God be so, that ye suffer for well doing, than for evil doing.

18 For Christ also hath once suffered for sins, the just for the unjust, that he might bring us to God, being put to death in the flesh, but quickened by the Spirit:

1 Corinthians 6: 1 – 10 King James Version

6 Dare any of you, having a matter against another, go to law before the unjust, and not before the saints?

² Do ye not know that the saints shall judge the world? and if the world shall be judged by you, are ye unworthy to judge the smallest matters?

³ Know ye not that we shall judge angels? how much more things that pertain to this life?

⁴ If then ye have judgments of things pertaining to this life, set them to judge who are least esteemed in the church.

⁵ I speak to your shame. Is it so, that there is not a wise man among you? No, not one that shall be able to judge between his brethren?

⁶ But brother goeth to law with brother, and that before the unbelievers.

⁷ Now therefore there is utterly a fault among you, because ye go to law one with another. **Why do ye not rather take wrong? Why do ye not rather suffer yourselves to be defrauded?**

⁸ Nay, ye do wrong, and defraud, and that your brethren.

⁹ Know ye not that the unrighteous shall not inherit the kingdom of God? Be not deceived: neither fornicators, nor idolaters, nor adulterers, nor effeminate, nor abusers of themselves with mankind,

¹⁰ Nor thieves, nor covetous, nor drunkards, nor revilers, nor extortioners, shall inherit the kingdom of God.

1 Peter 3:4

But let it be the hidden man of the heart, in that which is not corruptible, even the ornament of a **meek** and quiet spirit, which is in the sight of God of great price.

A meek and quiet spirit is of great price in the sight of God.

Numbers 12:3

(Now the man Moses was very **meek**, above all the men which were upon the face of the earth.)

Psalm 22:26

The **meek** shall eat and be satisfied: they shall praise the LORD that seek him: your heart shall live for ever.

Psalm 25:9

The **meek** will he guide in judgment: and the **meek** will he teach his way.

Psalm 37:11

But the **meek** shall inherit the earth; and shall delight themselves in the abundance of peace..

Psalm 147:6

The LORD lifteth up the **meek**: he casteth the wicked down to the ground.

Psalm 149:4

For the LORD taketh pleasure in his people: he will beautify the **meek** with salvation.

Isaiah 61:1

The Spirit of the Lord GOD is upon me; because the LORD hath anointed me to preach good tidings unto the **meek**; he hath sent me to bind up the brokenhearted, to proclaim liberty to the captives, and the opening of the prison to them that are bound;

Zephaniah 2:3

Seek ye the LORD, all ye **meek** of the earth, which have wrought his judgment; seek righteousness, seek **meek**ness: it may be ye shall be hid in the day of the LORD's anger.

Matthew 5:5

Blessed are the **meek**: for they shall inherit the earth.

Matthew 11:29

Take my yoke upon you, and learn of me; for I am **meek** and lowly in heart: and ye shall find rest unto your souls.

Matthew 21:5

Tell ye the daughter of Sion, Behold, thy King cometh unto thee, **meek**, and sitting upon an ass, and a colt the foal of an ass.

Colossians 3:12

Put on therefore, as the elect of God, holy and beloved, bowels of mercies, kindness, humbleness of mind, **meek**ness, longsuffering;

1 Timothy 6:11

But thou, O man of God, flee these things; and **follow after** righteousness, godliness, faith, love, patience, **meekness**.

[24] And the servant of the Lord must not strive; but be gentle unto all men, apt to teach, patient,

[25] In meekness instructing those that oppose themselves; if God peradventure will give them repentance to the acknowledging of the truth;

[26] And that they may recover themselves out of the snare of the devil, who are taken captive by him at his will.

Titus 3:2

To speak evil of no man, to be no brawlers, but gentle, shewing all **meek**ness unto all men.

James 3:13

Who is a wise man and endued with knowledge among you? let him shew out of a good conversation his works with **meek**ness of wisdom.

9. Temperance

The word "temperance" comes from the Greek words *en* and *kratos*. The word *en* means *in*, and the word *kratos* is the Greek word for *power*. When compounded into one word, these two Greek words form *egkrateia*, which literally means *in control* and denotes *power over one's self*. It suggests *the control or restraint of one's passions, appetites, and desires*.

A person with temperance maintains a life of *moderation* and *control*. Because the Holy Spirit has produced temperance in his life, he is able to say no to overeating, overworking, and overworrying. God's Spirit produces in him a discipline that helps him say no to *any* excesses in the physical realm. So the word *egkrateia*— "temperance"— could be translated as *restraint*, *moderation*, *discipline*, *balance*, *temperance*, or *self-control*.

https://www.bible.com/reading-plans/24593-the-fruit-of-the-spirit-by-rick-renner/day/6

It is saying 'no' to any legal thing done in excess, like overeating, overworking, etc.

It is being in control of one's passions and desires.

How do you apply temperance in real life?

Here is an example:

If you are a person who constantly find yourself overeating or cannot control your appetite when it comes to food, you combat this excessive eating by applying fasting and prayer. I am speaking about fasting without any form of food, just having water alone for a significant period of time.

I am closing this chapter with the following scripture verses.

2 Peter 1: 5 – 9

[5] And beside this, giving all diligence, add to your faith virtue; and to virtue knowledge;

⁶ And to knowledge temperance; and to temperance patience; and to patience godliness;

⁷ And to godliness brotherly kindness; and to brotherly kindness charity.

⁸ For **if these things be in you, and abound, they make you that ye shall neither be barren nor unfruitful in the knowledge of our Lord Jesus Christ.**

⁹ But he that lacketh these things is blind, and cannot see afar off, and hath forgotten that he was purged from his old sins.

John 15: 1 to 5 King James Version

15 I am the true vine, and my Father is the husbandman.

² Every branch in me that beareth not fruit he taketh away: and every branch that beareth fruit, he purgeth it, that it may bring forth more fruit.

³ Now ye are clean through the word which I have spoken unto you.

⁴ Abide in me, and I in you. As the branch cannot bear fruit of itself, except it abide in the vine; no more can ye, except ye abide in me.

⁵ I am the vine, ye are the branches: He that abideth in me, and I in him, the same bringeth forth much fruit: for without me ye can do nothing.

If you walk in the Spirit by demonstrating the fruit of the Spirit throughout each day, your spiritual eyes would be opened to see in the spirit, your spiritual ears would be opened to hear in the spirit, and all your spiritual senses would be activated.

12

Seeking the Lord

2 Chronicles 7:14 King James Version

If my people, which are called by my name, shall humble themselves, and **pray, and seek my face,** and turn from their wicked ways; then will I hear from heaven, and will forgive their sin, and will heal their land.

Psalm 27:8 King James Version

When thou saidst, Seek ye my face; my heart said unto thee, **Thy face, LORD, will I seek.**

How can the Lord tell us to seek His face in His Word and then not show us His face?

This is not figurative language but literal language.

We have wrongly translated it in our sermons for years to mean something figurative; when the Lord means it in a literal way.

Seek the Lord in prayer until….until you see His face.

Psalm 42:1, 2 King James Version

As the hart panteth after **the** water brooks, so panteth my soul after thee, O God.

My soul thirsteth for God, for the living God: when shall I come and appear before God?

Psalm 63:1 King James Version

O God, thou art **my** God; early will I seek thee: **my soul thirsteth for thee, my flesh longeth for thee** in a dry and thirsty land, where no water is;

Psalm 143:6 King James Version

I stretch forth **my** hands unto thee: my soul thirsteth **after thee,** as a thirsty land. Selah.

Jeremiah 29:13 King James Version

And ye **shall seek me,** and **find me** when ye shall search for **me** with all **you**r heart.

Isaiah 55:6 King James Version

⁶ Seek ye the L̲o̲r̲d̲ while He may be found, call ye upon Him while He is near:

Do you seek Him with all your heart?

Seeking Him with all your heart is having your entire being consumed with thoughts and feelings about Him and for Him, all the time.

Are you passionate for Him like this?

Do you long for Him like this?

Do you seek Him like this?

Do you desire Him like this?

How long do you seek Him for?

You seek Him until…until you find Him. Until He reveals Himself to you, Until you see Him, Until you become close to Him. And when you have become close to Him, you don't stop seeking Him, but you continue to seek Him to know Him more and more, since it would take you all of eternity and more of seeking Him to get to know Him.

When I was 17 years old, I felt strongly impressed in my spirit to seek the Lord till I found Him, to become more intimate with and closer to the Lord Jesus Christ.

Although I was already saved since I was 7 years old, I still felt the need to know Him more, to become closer and closer to Him.

Initially, I decided to fast and pray for at least 30 days – setting apart at least 4 hours or more a day, every day, for 30 days straight, to seek Him on my knees in prayer for 4 straight hours every day for 30 days till He revealed Himself to me.

For the first 3 days of prayer and fasting, praying for 4 straight hours on my knees for those 3 days (I still prayed throughout the day, but this 4 hours was fully dedicated, set-apart time to seek Him). I felt nothing, except the pain in my knees after kneeling down for 4 straight hours.

In fact, I felt as dry as a biscuit. I felt as if my prayers were just hitting the ceiling of the room and falling down right before me.

But despite this, I did not stop praying, though, and because I persisted in prayer, I heard within my spirit, these words, "Don't seek the Lord Jesus Christ for anything, but to just love Him. Don't seek Him for a job, money, things, or make requests for Him to help someone during this time of prayer…not even to feel His presence. Just seek Him because you love Him. Only seek Him because you want to develop a love-relationship with Him…."

After I told Him I came not to ask Him for anything but just to tell Him how much I love Him, within minutes, His presence entered the room strongly. I felt Him so near. His presence was so strong that I felt like I was going to burst. I found myself weeping and weeping for a long time, for hours. And said, "Lord, if you don't turn this off I feel like I am going to burst…"

These experiences continued for days, weeks and months, until I got employed, then my quality time that I once spent with Him was now greatly limited.

Jeremiah 29:13 King James Version

And ye **shall seek me**, **and find me** when ye shall search for me with all your heart.

He has promised that if we seek Him we shall find Him but only when we seek Him with all our heart.

Let us make a never-ending commitment to seek Him till we find Him, and to continue to seek Him to know Him.

So let's make our seeking Him twofold:

1. Let's seek Him to find Him. He is not the One who moved away from us, we are the ones who moved away from Him.

2. After we reconnect with Him through our initial seeking of Him we must then seek Him to know Him, to become intimate with Him, to become one with Him, experientially. It is important to not only have a head-knowledge of Him, but also practical, life-experiences with Him.

Chapter 13

How do I know if what I am hearing and seeing is from God or not?

All prophecies, visions, trances, revelations from the spirit realm, must line up with the Word of God. They must be verified and established in the mouth of two or three witnesses in the Holy Bible. If you cannot find scripture verses to back up your spiritual experiences they either originated from your own soul, or came directly from the enemy.

Matthew 18:16

But if he will not hear thee, then take with thee one **or two** more, that in the mouth of two or three witnesses every word may be established.

2 Corinthians 13:1

This is the third time I am coming to you. In the mouth of **two or three** witnesses shall every word be established.

If you cannot find two or more scriptural references

in the bible to confirm what you or someone else giving you a 'word from the Lord' have heard or witnessed in the spiritual realm concerning you, then more than likely what was heard or seen came from the soulish area or from the enemy.

There are 3 ways to determine if what you saw or heard from the spirit realm is from God or the devil:

1. You must have at least two or more scriptural references from the bible to confirm what you have heard or seen is from God.

2. The inner voice of the Holy Spirit will witness to you whether that word of prophecy, dream, vision or revelation was from God. .

3. Ask the Lord in prayer to confirm if it is from Him.

For instance, the first time I saw my wife at church, (this is before I ever knew her) I heard a voice distinctly saying to me, "She will be your wife".

After receiving that Rhema word from the Lord, I sought Him in prayer for 17 consecutive years or 6,205 days, asking Him for confirmation several times during each one of those 6,205 days.

(365 days per year x 17 years x how many times I prayed each day to get confirmation from God).

I actually prayed thousands of times to ensure that I was making the right decision when it came to marriage. And believe it or not, each time the Lord confirmed to me that she would be my wife.

So I literally had (without exaggerating), more than 6,205 confirmations from God that she would be my wife. But even though I had all these confirmations concerning my wife to be – I never shared or discussed it with anyone but God.

How I was able to do that only God alone knows. It had to be His strength that helped me.

Did this word from the Lord came to pass easily without the enemy trying his best to stop it?

No, it did not.

Because even though I had all those confirmations from the Lord, I cannot relate to you here all the tests, trials and persecutions I went through concerning that word from the Lord, but because the Lord confirmed to me thousands of times that she would be my wife I was wholly convinced, and nothing could have swayed me from believing that word, the prophetic dreams and visions which I heard and saw from the Lord, Himself, to verify that she would be my wife.

I never knew, though, I would have had to wait that long, pray to receive so many confirmations from the Lord, or go through so much before that word came to pass.

This is why when God gives you a prophetic word or vision concerning the future of your life, most of the times, He never shares with you all the details of it.

Anyhow, I hope you are encouraged by part of my testimony here. You may not have to go through what I did. God was preparing me for something more than marriage, this is the major reason why I had to go through what I did.

All in all, what I am saying is:

"If you received a prophetic word or vision from the Lord concerning some area of your life, whether it is concerning marriage, ministry or otherwise, make sure you receive lots of confirmations from the Lord that what you heard and saw was from Him.

Wait before Him in prayer, listening to hear His voice clearly confirming that what you heard or saw was from Him."

There is much more I could say about this subject but I would have to leave that for another time.

Chapter 14
Pray these Prayers

By praying the inspired prayers found in the book of Ephesians and Colossians, often, throughout each day, you can have your spiritual eyes opened.

I would actually advise you to memorize these prayers and repeat them frequently throughout the day.

However, if you have skipped the previous chapters and jumped almost immediately to this chapter to pray these prayers because you want to avoid having to do all which had been written in the previous chapters – Go back to the first chapter of this book and read this book in the order which it was written.

There is no shortcut when it comes to the things of God.

Anyhow, I have taken the inspired prayers found in the books of Ephesians and Colossians and I have personalized them for myself to pray, often.

Don't worry, I have included those personalized prayers below for you. So that you too can use them in your prayer time.

Ephesians And Colossians Prayers

Ephesians 1: 17 - 23

The Amplified Bible Translation, Classic, Version

¹⁷ I thank you Heavenly Father, God of our Lord Jesus Christ, Father of glory, I thank You for giving me the spirit of wisdom and revelation…insight into your mysteries and secrets, in the [deep and intimate] knowledge of you,

¹⁸ cause the eyes of my heart, Heavenly Father, to be flooded with light, so that I can
know *and* understand the hope to which You have called me, and how rich is Your glorious inheritance in the saints is (Your set-apart ones),

19 Thank you for helping me to know and

understand Heavenly Father what is the immeasurable and unlimited *and* surpassing greatness of Your power in *and* for me who believe, as demonstrated in the working of Your mighty strength,

[20] Which You exerted in Christ when You raised Him from the dead and seated Him at Your [own] right hand in the heavenly [places],

[21] Far above all rule and authority and power and dominion and every name that is named [above every title that can be conferred], not only in this age *and* in this world, but also in the age *and* the world which are to come.

[22] And You have put all things under His feet and has appointed Him the universal and supreme Head of the church [a headship exercised throughout the church],

[23] Which is His body, the fullness of Him Who fills all in all [for in that body lives the full measure of Him

Who makes everything complete, and Who fills everything, everywhere with Himself.

Colossians Prayer:

Colossians 1: 9 – 12

The Amplified Bible Translation, Classic, Version

⁹ Heavenly Father, I thank you for filling me with the full (deep and clear) knowledge of Your will in all spiritual wisdom [in comprehensive insight into Your ways and purposes] and in understanding and discerning of spiritual things.

¹⁰ Thank you Heavenly Father for helping me to walk (live and conduct myself) in a manner worthy of You Lord, fully pleasing to You *and* [j]desiring to please You in all things, bearing fruit in every good work and steadily growing *and* increasing in *and* by the knowledge of You [with fuller, deeper, and clearer insight, [k]acquaintance, and recognition of You, Your will and Your purposes and plans].

¹¹ Thank you for invigorating *and* strengthening me with all power according to the might of Your glory, [to exercise] every kind of endurance and patience (perseverance and forbearance) with joy,

¹² thank you Heavenly Father, for qualifying me *and* making me fit to share the [l]portion which is the inheritance of the saints (God's holy people) in the Light.

You can also ask God to allow you to see visions and to have accurate and detailed dreams and revelations like Isaiah, Ezekiel, Jeremiah, Daniel and Joseph in the Bible.

God has promised to give you the desires of your heart.

And the Lord Jesus Christ, Himself, has said in John 15:7

If you abide in me and my words abide in you, you shall ask what you will and it shall be done unto you.

Question 1:

Do you know what the words of the Lord Jesus Christ are?

Do you meditate on them?

They are the words in the gospels in the Bible, Matthew, Mark, Luke, John and the words found in the book of Revelation which are highlighted in red in most bibles.

Do you meditate on these words day and night until you memorize them, and until they become embedded in your spirit?

The Lord Jesus has promised that if you abide in Him and His words abide in you, then you would be able to ask what you will and it shall be done unto you.

What's are the requirements for getting what you ask of Him in prayer?

They are:

    1. Abiding in Him

2. Having His words abide in you.
3. And being obedient to His Word.

How do you meditate on the Word?

How do you meditate on Jesus' words?

You read, listen and repeat them to yourself over and over and over again (particularly the words which the Lord Jesus Christ spoke in the gospels), until you not only memorize it, but it actually enters into your soul and spirit.

1 John 3: 22 – 24 King James Version

22 And whatsoever we ask, we receive of him, because we keep his commandments, and do those things that are pleasing in his sight.

23 And this is his commandment, That we should believe on the name of his Son Jesus Christ, and love one another, as he gave us commandment.

24 And he that keepeth his commandments

dwelleth in him, and he in him. And hereby we know that he abideth in us, by the Spirit which he hath given us.

Question 2:

Do you know if you do those things which are pleasing in His sight, you can ask Him for whatsoever you will and He will give it to you?

So, here is how these scriptures verses relate to 'seeing in the Spirit':

When you make a habit of meditating on the Word of God, particularly the words which the Lord Jesus Christ spoke in the gospels (Matthew, Mark, Luke and John), then you can ask what you will and it will be done for you.

Do you know you can also ask God to allow you to see visions, and to have accurate and detailed dreams and revelations like Isaiah, Ezekiel, Jeremiah, Daniel and Joseph in the Bible had and

He will hear and answer you **once you abide in Him, and His words abide in you?**

Do you know when you **make a habit of obeying the Word of God, and doing those things which please the Heavenly Father, daily,** you can ask Him to allow you to see visions, and to have accurate and detailed dreams and revelations like Isaiah, Ezekiel, Jeremiah, Daniel and Joseph in the Bible had and He will hear and answer you?

In summary:

- a. Abide in Him
- b. Meditate on His Word, daily
- c. Obey His Word and do those things which are pleasing in His sight.
- d. Ask Him for what you will and He will do it for you.
- e. Ask Him to see visions. Ask Him to give you prophetic dreams. Ask Him to see in the spirit realm. Ask Him to activate all your spiritual senses.

Printed in Great Britain
by Amazon